Everybody ^ELSE^ Is
Perfect

Everybody (Else) Is Perfect

How I Survived Hypocrisy, Beauty, Clicks, and Likes

GABRIELLE KORN

ATRIA PAPERBACK

New York   London   Toronto   Sydney   New Delhi

This publication is a memoir. It reflects the author's present recollections of her experiences over a period of years. Some names and identifying characteristics of individuals have been changed. Some dialogue has been re-created from memory. Some scenes are composites of events. Events have been compressed and in some cases their chronology has been changed.

An Imprint of Simon & Schuster, Inc.
1230 Avenue of the Americas
New York, NY 10020

First Atria Paperback edition January 2021

ATRIA PAPERBACK and colophon are trademarks of Simon & Schuster, Inc.

For information about special discounts for bulk purchases, please contact Simon & Schuster Special Sales at 1-866-506-1949 or business@simonandschuster.com.

The Simon & Schuster Speakers Bureau can bring authors to your live event. For more information or to book an event, contact the Simon & Schuster Speakers Bureau at 1-866-248-3049 or visit our website at www.simonspeakers.com.

Interior design by A. Kathryn Barrett

Manufactured in the United States of America

1   3   5   7   9   10   8   6   4   2

Library of Congress Cataloging-in-Publication Data
Names: Korn, Gabrielle, 1989– author.
Title: Everybody else is perfect : how I survived hypocrisy, beauty, clicks, and likes / Gabrielle Korn.
Other titles: Everybody is perfect
Description: First Atria Paperback edition. | New York : Atria Paperback, 2020.
Identifiers: LCCN 2019057651 (print) | LCCN 2019057652 (ebook) | ISBN 9781982127763 (paperback) | ISBN 9781982127787 (ebook)
Subjects: LCSH: Korn, Gabrielle, 1989– | Korn, Gabrielle, 1989—Anecdotes. | Women journalists—United States—Biography. | Lesbians—United States—Biography.
Classification: LCC PN4874.K667 A3 2020 (print) | LCC PN4874.K667 (ebook) | DDC 818/.603 [B]—dc23
LC record available at https://lccn.loc.gov/2019057651
LC ebook record available at https://lccn.loc.gov/2019057652

ISBN 978-1-9821-2776-3
ISBN 978-1-9821-2778-7 (ebook)

For my sisters, literal and otherwise

Contents

Everybody $\overset{ELSE}{\wedge}$ Is Perfect

Prologue

Dear Readers,

For two chaotically busy, gloriously productive, high-profile years, I was the US editor in chief of an international, independent publication called *Nylon*—a promotion I got when I was twenty-eight, younger than any *Nylon* editor in chief before me, and definitely the only lesbian who'd ever been at the top of the masthead. I was, in fact, younger and gayer than all the female EICs at competing publications in New York City, which was a point of pride for me but also made me an outsider. People like me were not supposed to get promotions like that.

What's more, I was promoted on the same day the print magazine, which was in many ways beloved and iconic, folded. It was a terrifying task, but being put in a position of power meant that I could pour my idealism into something concrete:

institutional change. I loved the brand but saw its flaws very clearly, and I was committed to building an editorial strategy that prioritized racial diversity, that welcomed all bodies to the table, and that didn't limit the idea of coolness to a certain economic class.

Speaking of coolness: Growing up, I had been, in many ways, the kind of person for whom *Nylon* magazine was created, but I never felt like I was cool enough to read it. Like other magazines, it was so exclusive that it barely included anyone. As a teen in the early 2000s, I was an art kid who loved fashion but not in a popular-girl way, who self-identified as a music snob at fifteen, who dated skaters, who went to emo shows and played guitar in a punk band. *Nylon* was sold at Urban Outfitters, where I shopped; it partnered with Myspace, on which I spent my free time. It had always been in the background of my life. But as a queer woman, I also didn't see myself reflected in its pages, or really, any glossy magazine pages at all; even before I had words for my deepest desires, I felt that there was something inherent that rendered me *other*.

Maybe because of that, when I was younger, working as a magazine editor didn't even occur to me. I fluctuated between vague ambitions. Sometimes I wanted to be a painter or a photographer, other times a poet. But I also wanted to write articles, and as I tried to make a career around online journalism in my early twenties, the lifestyle publications were the ones that paid me. And as someone who cared a lot about my own physical appearance, I also turned out to be good at writing about aesthetics in a compelling way. I found myself pulled toward the vibrant, bustling world of New York City fashion media, as though it weren't a choice but an inevitability.

In my early days as a beauty editor, I was confronted by how a women's industry could be so obviously centered around, and controlled by, a straight, cisgender, white male gaze. I was astounded to watch my inbox fill every day with pitches from publicists about how to groom my body hair to please "my man"—I'd then watch as competing publications that had clearly gotten those same pitches would run stories using the same language. So, in turn, I began to churn out work about *not* shaving your body hair, among other things, and in general I became a very vocal, probably annoying, voice for change. What was the point, I asked myself, in working myself to the bone for big, fancy publications as a dyke if I wasn't going to try to make the content accessible for other queer people?

Eventually I went to *Nylon*, where I was a digital editor for three years before my final promotion to the top spot, which meant the people in charge were finally starting to listen to alternate viewpoints. It was a huge win not just for me but for everyone like me who didn't see themselves represented in mainstream media.

Behind the scenes, though, a very different story had unfolded.

I'd achieved something majorly shiny and glamorous, but

along the way, it hadn't been so pretty. At various times, I was underpaid, discriminated against, and sexually assaulted. And despite my fancy day jobs, in my personal life, I consistently behaved like a typical twentysomething: I was dating women who didn't treat me well, I was sleeping with women I shouldn't have, and I was struggling to figure out how to identify my own needs, which in turn made me a shitty person to be in any kind of relationship with. I smoked too much pot and didn't get enough sleep. I alienated people who loved me with my inability to ask for help and my tendency to self-isolate.

I was also trying, and failing, and trying again, to recover from anorexia, a secret struggle that impacted every single aspect of my life. In contrast with my personal brand, the hypocrisy of my diagnosis wasn't lost on me, and that was just one more reason for me to be filled with self-loathing. Once I had big, "important" jobs, I was more than happy to hide behind the busyness that came with them, rather than face my own demons.

I wanted so badly to show the world that an iconic fashion-based publication could become a beacon of thought leadership if you just let young women steer the ship. And we were very successful. I prioritized diversity within everything we made, and the brand evolved. Young readers called us "woke *Nylon*." My junior editors called me "Mom."

Eventually, I made a name for myself as a champion for inclusion. Work was still crazy, but by the end of my twenties, I was starting to get my emotional life together, falling in love with a woman who treated me with kindness and respect. I felt I knew myself. And then, in July 2019, two months after my thirtieth birthday, *Nylon* was suddenly acquired by a much larger company. I was caught completely off guard. I hadn't realized how burnt-out I was until that moment. I felt like I had nothing left to give, and so I resigned.

I had thrown myself fully into the work of making women's media safe for all kinds of bodies but had become almost disembodied in the process. I could power through exhaustion and starvation and high heels that tore up my feet, and justify it with how important the work would be to other people.

I'd been led to believe that notoriety is the ultimate aspiration, but the truth of the matter was I had been running a company as though it were mine when I didn't own a single piece of it. I had made positive change, but when you strip all the pretense away—the things our culture says make you an empowered woman—what's left? Who are we, as contemporary feminists, without capitalism?

I realized that without my fancy job title, I didn't know how to describe myself. And really, the question for all of us is this: As a new generation of women, how do we recognize ourselves and each other without the pressure to be perfect—however that's currently being defined?

I learned the hard way that professional success is not a good indicator of well-being. And I believe that is a deeply relatable phenomenon, though it's usually spoken in whispers, especially for women. So when I quit my big, fancy job, after spending a few weeks moping, I got to work. But it was a new kind of work, and the first step was returning to my own body. The second was remembering what it felt like to have ownership of my time. The third was deciding what to do with it.

I also, immediately, had a book to finish—you're holding it.

In the yearlong period between pitching the idea and finishing the manuscript, my life had been turned upside down. And I came out the other side stronger, and more self-aware, and with a clearer idea of what I needed. Suddenly, I had a much bigger story to tell.

This is a book about what happens when you put your own well-being on hold to achieve a version of success that you think you're supposed to want, and how I finally was able to see—and then escape—the confines of perfection. I hope you enjoy the ride.

Gabrielle

1

The Beautiful Flaw

In early 2013, a few months before I turned twenty-four, I landed a job as a production assistant in the beauty department of a rapidly growing digital media company for women called Refinery29. The job itself (building posts in the back end and photo research, mostly) wasn't exactly a dream, but the company was: a newly notable fashion site defined by superiorly cool taste, it was trying to become the world's destination for style. I didn't know too much about fashion, but I loved clothes and makeup. I'd been writing for *Autostraddle*—an online magazine for queer women—for a little over a year and had gotten lucky: the woman I sent my resume to was familiar with the website and had been interested in improving the diversity of the beauty department. As a lesbian, I was a diverse hire. It was also good timing—a few months after I started, the company strategy shifted and our department went from being responsible for five stories a day to around twenty. My editors, grateful for my youthful enthusiasm, quickly gave me more responsibilities, and eventually I was writing stories all day on hair, makeup, skin care, and nails.

The intense increase in article production was helmed by a hardworking, talented editorial team that was willing to be experimental at a time when the competition was playing it safe, and it worked. Like, *really* worked. Soon there was a site-wide traffic boom so enormous it seemed like every week we were champagne-toasting a new milestone. We sailed past ten million unique readers per month and continued to climb. The offices moved from one large room in the East Village to two entire floors of a skyscraper in the Financial District. A huge flat-screen TV was mounted on the wall in the editorial department so that Chartbeat, a dashboard that shows you in real time how many people are on your site, was always visible.

The brand gained name recognition in the industry, and the writers were getting noticed, too, literally: I was regularly stopped on the street by young women who recognized me from my byline photo and DIY videos. It was thrilling; there was a large part of me that always doubted I could become a successful writer, and the attention was flattering and addictive. Beauty brands started flying me around the world—I went to Singapore to cover a skin-care brand, Milan for the launch of Gucci makeup, Nashville when Carrie Underwood became a makeup spokesperson, Paris for a new hair dye innovation. Even though I was still an assistant, telling people where I worked would elicit a breathless "Oh!"

Then, of course, the numbers plateaued. We scrambled, working all hours of the night to be the first to cover a Kardashian hair change or announce the launch of a new Urban Decay Naked Palette. It wasn't working. Even though we were maintaining, not losing traffic, a sense of defeat hung in the air. Chartbeat, which had so recently set the room aglow with success, now loomed above us, a constant reminder of how we'd slowed.

Digital media, especially at that time, was an endless roller coaster dictated by clicks, and it was difficult to tell from one day to the next which stories would take off and which would die upon publication. This was the beginning of social media's reign of terror over the industry. Suddenly the way a link was posted on Facebook, and when, would be the difference in tens of thousands of visits. But it didn't seem like an institutional problem yet—instead of criticizing the system, we pointed fingers at each other, and ourselves. It wasn't uncommon to try to find a private place to cry, like a stairwell, only to find someone already there doing the same thing. There was one day when I wrote ten news posts in a row; by evening, my eyes felt like they were bleeding. There were many people who were writing even more than me. In hindsight, I have no idea how we did it.

In this liminal space without strategy, there was a unique opportunity: we were encouraged to try just about anything. No pitch was too crazy. First person seemed to work well for our competitors (it was, after all, the middle of the first-person essay boom, also commonly referred to online as the first-person industrial complex), so we all started digging deep into our own psyches. Eventually I turned out a story called "People Have a Lot of Feelings about You Not Shaving." By "you," I meant me: I wrote about my high school guidance counselor telling me not to apply to a small liberal arts college in western Massachusetts because it was filled with "hairy lesbians," and how though I didn't apply, I grew up to be one anyway. I talked about the reactions I got when people noticed my various body hair—hostile stares on the subway, an uncomfortable check-in with a former boss about what's appropriate for an office setting. Strangers told me I looked like a man. Well-meaning acquaintances often asked to touch it.

This was around the time that "no-makeup makeup" was becoming popular. Thanks to the Beyoncé song, people started tagging their selfies #wokeuplikethis to promote natural beauty and also, probably, to feel morally superior about it. In my self-righteous twenty-four-year-old words I proclaimed that there was a difference between natural beauty and radical beauty—that the former is a privilege for those who fit the standard, and the latter is about reclaiming the concept of beauty for identities that are usually excluded from it. The point was that it's possible to make a political statement with your grooming habits. Basically I was writing about queer signifiers for what was, at the time, a mainstream fashion website. It was something I felt particularly strongly about because I was extremely conflicted about launching a career in an industry I'd always felt excluded from: I was holding on tight to my identity, determined to not be erased. In the essay, I talked about how important it was for me to be seen, and how my long body hair juxtaposed with the short hair on my head gave me the visibility and validation I craved—which was as true in my new workplace as it had been in college. It went viral.

Soon everything I wrote was about alternative beauty, calling out the ways in which the industry was failing women by putting us in boxes. I felt like a feminist infiltrator, taking down the system from within. I wasn't alone: writers in different verticals experienced a similar trajectory. Those of us willing to expose our deepest selves, to use fashion and beauty as a window to talk about more serious issues, were rewarded with traffic and respect. It was "it happened to me" for millennials: the format made viral by xoJane combined with a second-wave personal-is-political ideology. Eventually, there was a mandate across editorial that everyone needed to start writing personal essays, and gradually our traffic was back up. I quickly learned that the up-and-down nature of web traffic was the norm, not just there but across the industry.

Because my most popular writing tended to be about redefining beauty standards, I was eventually asked to write a story that was to be called "My Beautiful Flaw." The idea, as explained to me, was to create an originally photographed slideshow and accompanying interviews of maybe seven to ten women, all of whom should have what other people might call a flaw but from which they derived a sense of empowerment or specialness. "Like someone with two different-colored eyes," the assigning editor told me.

Getting such a major assignment at my level was a huge opportunity, but the task of casting for the story filled me with anxiety. Who was I to decide what constituted a flaw? And many of the women I initially reached out to were so offended by the question ("You think my hair/nose/skin is a flaw?" was, not surprisingly, the usual response) that I had to change the wording entirely, even though I knew the final headline would probably have to be what the editor originally wanted.

Then there was an added layer of trouble: I easily found dozens of women with some sort of standout feature, like a very visible scar, or prematurely gray hair, or some asymmetry, all of whom were roundly rejected. It quickly became clear that every woman featured, while being lauded for her "flaw," still had to be conventionally attractive and trendy. "Can't you just find, like, a model with one blue eye and one green eye?" was the feedback. Eventually I put an ad on Craigslist and was flooded with responses. I contacted agencies; I had all my friends reach out to all their friends. I started to become familiar with what would get rejected ahead of time—no matter how remarkable someone's scar was, if she wasn't also classically pretty and hipster cool, it was a no. I was overwhelmed with both guilt and powerlessness.

The whole thing started to feel like a round peg in a square hole. What's the point of celebrating differences if you're going to put parameters around just how different they're allowed to be? The implicit message was, It's okay to have something weird about you, as long as, overall, you're easy on the eyes. I started to realize that this probably applied to my own editorial success. Sure, I had short pink hair and fuzzy calves, but I was also white, skinny, and young, and my clothes were cute. My aesthetic differences were just quirks.

Eventually, after I left, the company would pivot their content to champion both racial and size diversity—though internally, it would struggle for a long time to develop a work culture that matched the new mission of the editorial. But in the era of "My Beautiful Flaw," most mainstream fashion publications, digital or print, were still predominantly filled with images of thin white women. Despite my queerness, I was just another one of them. I understood that as a white Jewish lesbian, the parts of my identity that might marginalize me were largely invisible; I was benefiting from the system while being tokenized by it.

In the end it took six months to get just three women approved for the story, and we decided to cap it at that, before I lost my mind. I convinced my editors to let me change the headline to "Why Beauty Isn't about Being Perfect," which was still mildly offensive to the women featured, but less potentially devastating. Of the three, one was a runway model with albinism, one was an activist with vitiligo, and one was a writer with a delicate scar down the middle of her face. All of them were beautiful. And despite the headline, they were all pretty much perfect, too.

I was praised by my peers for the final result but was so jaded by the process that I couldn't tell if I had actually done anything for the greater good. And while the story ended up trafficking fairly well, several readers' comments indicated they had picked up on what I had: that even though the content claimed to be promoting alternative beauty, it wasn't really doing all that much to further the cause; the women featured didn't actually deviate all too strongly from the norm. A few readers told me off-line that while they appreciated the concept, it felt like an obvious, cheap "get," part of a larger plot to take advantage of how desperate women are to see themselves reflected in the media they consume and use it as a business growth strategy. That was, of course, my worst nightmare. I'd been so passionate about improving representation, and the fact that it was seen as anything other than earnest was a painful but important lesson: there are always ways to do better.

This story would have been easy to cast a few years later, thanks to the rise of alternative influencers on Instagram: beautiful teens with hundreds of thousands of followers started posting images of their cystic acne, or unibrow, or back rolls, with long captions about how scary and vulnerable it was to share those parts of themselves, inspiring others to do the same. But I'm not sure a roundup of them would make for appropriate content.

If the goal is to embrace your uniqueness, putting people into categories—normatively attractive or, well, not—feels at odds.

But this was 2013, 2014. All kinds of brands were starting to adopt a similar tactic at the same time. Inclusivity and diversity became an aesthetic, and across the industry, people noticed that the top performing stories all dealt with some sort of outrage: on the heels of a social justice callout culture that originated on Tumblr, hot takes reigned supreme. Thanks to comment sections, readers were holding digital properties to a certain set of values that they'd never been accountable for before, and publishers who could fulfill those demands seemed to fare the best. It turned into a race to be the first to point out the problematic nature of a movie, show, commercial, ad campaign—you name it. It was equal parts thrilling and stressful: sometimes it felt like the more woke we were, the more people picked us apart, which was ultimately good—it meant we were constantly checking ourselves.

Behind the scenes, though, very few companies had staffs that reflected the values they pushed. At major magazines in the mainstream media, there was a definite shift to more diverse content, but the writers and editors remained, for the most part, white, cis, straight, and so, so thin. (Not to mention the fact that the owners of women's media companies were usually men.)

In hindsight, it was a major problem indicative of something much larger that the most visible body-positive, diverse content was largely being touted by a group of people who weren't really any of those things. It's as if they were saying, "It's okay for *you*, the reader, to be any size, to do whatever you want with your body hair, to style yourself in a way that makes you feel good; but we must maintain our standards."

The implication, overall, is that diversity was just another trend, with media executives choosing to wait it out.

Of course, in reality, this disconnect was largely due to the fact that progressive editorial teams had little to no say in things like hiring, and most of them were doing the best they could with limited resources. And, culturally, we're all products of the values of the generation that came before us, trying to function and succeed in a society that has, up until now, basically told women that we're not good enough. Not thin enough, not cute enough. It's hard to shake that messaging; when you grow up surrounded by it, it becomes part of your internal landscape.

The best that most of us can do is change the messaging for the next generation. *We* might never stop feeling as though if we just lost that ten pounds, or had that scar removed, or got rid of our gray hair / wrinkles / sun spots, we'd be happier, but maybe if we start leaving the discourse of physical flaws out of content entirely, it'll die when we do.

2

Staying Out

I'd felt an attraction to other girls for as long as I could remember, but up until I was a teenager I thought that everyone did. At fifteen, I made out with my best friend on a dare, and she pulled away with a perfunctory "ew," wiping her mouth, and it felt like my heart was being run over by a Mack truck.

She was definitely the coolest person in the entire world, and she'd picked *me* to be her best friend. She was punk before anyone else we knew, dying her curly black hair every color of the rainbow, arranging safety pins and aggressively political patches throughout all of her belongings. We had sleepovers almost every weekend. We'd get intentionally stuck in thunderstorms in the mall parking lot and then spend hours aimlessly walking through the aisles of Tower Records, documenting every moment on disposable cameras, however mundane, because everything—to me—felt like magic.

I had always flirted and been affectionate not just with her but all my friends, and they'd started to give me suspicious looks if I took it too far. At crew practice, a popular girl whispered in my ear that she wanted to hook up with me, and I was so convinced it was a trap that it made me cry. Someone I'd been friends with started an email chain saying, in lewd teenager terms, that I acted like I wanted to have a dick.

At sixteen, I started "dating" a close friend from childhood who lived four hours away (my family had moved from Rhode Island to New York when I was eleven, and we'd stayed in touch). He was sweet, shy, and artistic. We'd spend hours on the phone or chatting on AIM throughout middle school, and once we were teenagers, the feelings turned to something more. We started taking the train to see each other every couple of months. I genuinely liked him a lot, and hanging out every few weeks felt like just the right amount of commitment. Things got physical, and eventually we lost our virginities to each other, which was a tender moment but ultimately very anticlimactic for me, literally and emotionally. Being sexually active was confusing: I liked the attention and the affection, but it felt so . . . empty. Within a few months, I tumbled into a deep depression so overwhelming that I accidentally stopped speaking to him. He broke up with me over the landline apologetically, saying he assumed it was what I wanted based on my behavior. I cried a lot, but not really for the relationship. There was something bigger that I didn't have words for. I remember that I kept thinking, on repeat, *What the fuck is wrong with me?*

After that I always had boys around, most of whom I think I did like, but I would become repulsed by them as soon as they actually became my boyfriend, which made my peers think I was kind of slutty—a safe, convenient reputation considering what was really going on with me. If they thought I was a slut, they wouldn't think I was something else.

The public school I went to was wildly homophobic. Maybe it was a reflection of the times, but the few out gay kids—and the closeted ones, for that matter—were mercilessly bullied. I'd find out years later that a group of kids a few grades above me had a running bet about whether or not I was gay, which was undoubtedly the worst thing you could be, aside from unattractive. There was no such thing as learning about queer people and their contributions to society in a curriculum. So it's no wonder that the word "lesbian" didn't fully materialize for me, mostly because there were no other lesbians around me to look up to, in real life or in the media I consumed. I was well aware that I had major, intensely physical crushes on girls—I even talked about it with my older sister Miriam—but it felt totally separate from who I was, a subtext that I didn't realize informed the plot. I thought maybe I was just bad at sex. Everyone else seemed to really like it.

By senior prom, there was basically no one left for me to

date or even make out with, and I went alone. I remember sitting in the kitchen in my shiny satin pink dress while my parents took pictures of my twin sister, Julia, and her boyfriend in the front hallway, refusing to join them so that my solitude wouldn't be documented.

Another girl without a date in my group of friends was Kat, who had grown up around the corner from me. We'd formed a punk band in seventh grade and since then she had always been a solid presence in my life, often coming over just to sit on my floor and quietly play guitar. Kat was always butch, but we didn't talk about it until we were in our twenties. After prom, in the house we'd all rented together for the weekend, while everyone else was off having sex, she and I sat on the porch and she taught me how to smoke pot out of a three-foot bong. We were stoned when the sun came up, and I'm pretty sure I ate a whole bag of chips.

High school had been hard for me for a lot of different reasons. I was never what you might call an enthusiastic student. I wanted to paint and write and play my guitar and listen to music. Anything else felt, truly, like a waste of time. I didn't understand why I had to do homework when I had already sat in class all day. I felt both smarter than everyone and like the dumbest person in the room, hopelessly failing chemistry and math tests but always impressing my English and history teachers. Eventually I realized that if I did absolutely zero studying, I could still get by in honors classes with A minuses and Bs, so I stopped trying, coasting along with medium success and often going to great lengths to hide my grades from my parents. Getting accepted into my first-choice college, NYU's Gallatin School of Individualized Study, was probably thanks to my surprisingly high test scores and out-of-the-box extracurriculars, *not* my underwhelming academic accomplishments.

The individualized educational route was not an accident; by then I knew my learning style could best be defined as fueled by passion—I simply couldn't wrap my head around things that felt irrelevant, like calculus. I didn't feel like failing any more math or science classes, so instead I chose the option where I never had to take them again. I was desperate for intellectual freedom, which I got, but that meant there were *no* guidelines. In the absence of a curriculum, I spent my freshman year floundering. I took classes simply because they sounded cool, on topics like ethnomusicology and semantics, without any real plan. Every time someone asked me what I'd mold my major into, I made up a different answer. I was learning a lot, to be sure, but about so many different things at once that it felt nearly impossible to imagine a career. I figured maybe I'd be a professor, if anything.

My social life was floundering, too. As much as I'd longed for independence, as it turned out, I was also terrified of new people. For the first month of college I clung to my high school friends who were also at NYU (a popular choice for Long Islanders), and Miriam, who had moved to Manhattan after her own undergraduate experience. I didn't want to go home, though. Even though my parents were only an hour away, it was hard to reconcile my newfound freedom with the boundaries of my childhood home, and being there made me moody and anxious. I think I didn't want to be reminded that at eighteen, I was still very much a kid.

One night I came home to find a girl I hadn't seen before sitting outside of my dorm room, eating cereal from the box. She had wild curly red ringlets framing a sweet, freckled face. Next to her, a little too close, was a stony-looking boy wearing a drug rug who she clearly had no interest in talking to. I introduced myself and we discovered we had similar names, though she went by Gabby, and we exchanged numbers on our flip phones, making a plan to hang out the next day. We quickly became best, best, *BEST* friends, spending all of our time together, eschewing any sort of social networking imposed by the school in order to have NYC adventures on our own. Being friends with Gabby was the easiest thing I'd ever done. We were so similar it felt like hanging out with an additional sister. She taught me how to smoke pot from a bowl (I never wanted to see a three-foot bong again), often lighting the weed for me because I was scared of getting burned. Eventually we each made a few separate acquaintances, but generally we were a package deal.

I was also clinging tightly to heterosexuality, because I had a very specific idea of what my life should look like in college, and it involved a boyfriend. There was no real reasoning behind that idea other than I was convinced it was what I should do. I was hooking up with guys constantly, waiting for it to feel like *something*, but instead I just felt more and more empty. I was drinking a lot, too, and many of those encounters I barely remembered. I became increasingly out of control, a rapid downward spiral of booze and strange boys. My friendship with Gabby and the proximity of my sister were my lifelines. We kept track of each other.

At the end of our freshman year I decided to stay in the city for the summer. I was acting like a feral cat; going home to Long Island after two semesters of total freedom was unimaginable. Plus, I was busy: I'd gotten an internship at an indie record label in Williamsburg and a night gig working the door at a music venue in Alphabet City. The internship, like most, was unpaid. But at night, the aging, mullet-haired venue manager was often so coked out that he'd toss several stacks of twenties at me, laughing and saying, "How much am I supposed to pay you? Whatever, here!" I'd get home at three a.m. and show up puffy and greasy to the office at nine the next morning, where my intern supervisor—who had hooked me up with the venue gig—would tease, "You're the hardest-working teenager in the music industry."

I moved to the NYU summer dorms a few blocks east, into a suite with three bedrooms and six girls total. My new roommate was a psychology major who blushed when she laughed, named Lucy. She had short, wheat-blonde hair; huge, doleful pale-blue eyes; and an oversize labret piercing. She was very feminine but wore no makeup, so she had kind of an earthy vibe. She was shy and spoke softly with a subtle Tennessee twang. She was, frankly, the first out lesbian I'd ever gotten to know. After a few days of intense, manic friendship, during which we ate dumplings and watched *Buffy* on my laptop, I nervously told her I thought maybe I was bi.

Lucy replied with an eye roll and a sigh. She said, "Straight girls always say that to lesbians," shutting down the conversation before it even started.

Sometimes I'd catch her smiling at me across our small kitchen table while we smoked pot out of a hookah and ate takeout with our other roommates, everyone in tank tops and cutoff shorts, barefoot and high and sweating, the air thick with our teenage summer smells. One night, a couple of weeks after I'd moved in, she texted me to come meet her at a nearby party because she was too drunk to walk home alone. I picked her up around two a.m., and we held hands on the way back to the dorm. I was wearing a short black dress, combat boots, and oversize black plastic glasses with no lenses. It was drizzling lightly. When we got back, I turned the lights out, and we got into our separate beds. A few minutes later she wordlessly got into mine. My heart was pounding so hard I thought maybe she could hear it. I wasn't sure if she was just making an alcohol-induced decision, and I certainly didn't want to cross any boundaries, so I lay as still as possible. Eventually, she kissed me.

Time slowed down and then it sped up. Within a matter of days, I was telling everyone I knew that I had a girlfriend. It all happened so quickly, the previous two semesters of drunken hookups immediately fading into the background, with my new gay life and all of its possibilities shimmering all around me.

I had just turned nineteen and for the first time was catching a glimpse of what it might feel like to live on my own terms. Gabby was one of the first people I told. I called her from a bench in Washington Square Park on a warm afternoon toward the end of May, and I remember her saying, "I'm so jealous! I want to like a girl, too!" I knew it wasn't just about liking one girl, though. There was an ancient yearning just waiting to break free. I think that if I had met a woman I was attracted to who liked me back any sooner, I would have come out then; it really was just a matter of my feelings being validated by someone else.

I immediately cut off all my hair.

Coming out felt like waking up from a bad dream. I was *thrilled* to finally have a reason why I'd spent most of my life lonely and unhappy. As a lesbian, I was no longer doomed to always be an outsider. There were people who I was attracted to *who would also be attracted to me.*

It felt like the best news of my life—there was nothing wrong with me; I was just super fucking gay, and there were others out there like me. But when I told my parents, they were shocked. Turns out all the work I'd done to bury my true self—my fixation on having a boyfriend, for starters—was very convincing. They questioned my political motivation, asking me if it was because I hated men. They expressed concern at what seemed to be a choice that would make my life harder. They were worried about me, which I now know came from a place of love, but all I could see at the time was how incredibly painful it was to be met with disbelief when I was, for the first time in my whole life, actually sure of something.

My highs and lows became extreme: euphoria with my new girlfriend in our East Village dorm room, and phone calls with my parents during which we'd all sob. I worried about not being lovable, and I felt I needed to be perfect in order to keep the attention of another woman. I was so used to unrequited feelings that I couldn't quite believe she was attracted to me, and I was determined to make myself into the ideal person. But what was an "ideal" lesbian, really? The only lesbians on television were so impossibly thin and chic. Desperate for friends who would fully understand what I was going through, I showed up to an event put on by the university's LGBTQ organization but left in tears; absolutely no one talked to me. They didn't even make eye contact. They also seemed to all already know one another, and stood in clusters, their tattoos and undercuts and piercings standing out in stark contrast to my boring brown pixie cut. Did I need to be more like them? What was I supposed to look like? How was I supposed to act? I'd never felt so uncool in my life.

The stress of coming out at nineteen in 2008 was a convenient excuse to turn down solids for long enough to achieve the sort of androgynously emaciated silhouette that all the dykes were going for in the aughts, special thanks to *The L Word*. I regularly had to buy smaller and smaller pants. I had no other reference for how to be attractive. I remember Lucy saying, "You're disappearing," while touching my ribs, her eyebrows furrowed with worry. But it felt like a compliment: I wanted to disappear, though I was unable to separate the metaphor from the reality of it.

Finally, feeling that conversations with my parents about my relationship were no longer productive, I sent them a long, emotional email asking them to accept me as I was. They didn't write back, but after that, they made a concerted effort to ask questions, and listen, and get to know my girlfriend (and girlfriends after that). It was a longer process than I would have liked, but ultimately I'm extremely lucky; within a couple of years, they both came around completely, understanding that it was neither a phase nor a choice. It helped that they weren't ever actually homophobic, just so deeply surprised that it took them time to adjust to the new reality. I take some responsibility for that: I hadn't told them about any of my crushes on girls growing up, or about the fact that I hated sex with boys (because, like, why would I tell them that? They're my parents). They eventually became more supportive than I ever could have imagined, taking it upon themselves to learn about queer culture and to integrate my identity into their understanding of their own. They even watched every season of *The L Word*.

I felt lucky to have such a supportive best friend, too, especially since a handful of other friends had stopped talking to me altogether—mostly guys. And my friends from Long Island had heard about it before I'd gotten the chance to tell them myself, so I knew I was the subject of gossip, which felt awful. But with Gabby there wasn't a single second of awkwardness. This new part of my life was an uncomplicated truth. My two sisters were also on board; Miriam was unofficially staying with us in my dorm when all of this went down, and so she got to witness the early stages of romance, which was nice for me—I didn't have to explain anything to her. Julia was equally supportive, just, as my twin, hurt that I'd never talked to her about it before.

At the end of June, Lucy took me to my first gay pride parade. It was pouring rain, and we both wore dresses, huddled together under a small umbrella. We squeezed our way to the front of the crowd in the West Village, watching as hundreds of people in various states of undress danced by. I had never seen so many queer people in my entire life. I don't think I had even realized there *were* that many queer people.

In September, Gabby and I moved into new dorms with randomly assigned roommates, one of whom came out a few weeks after we moved in together, and they became my other closest friend. Within a few months, Lucy and I broke up. I'd realized that just because I'd been physically attracted to her didn't mean we were actually compatible long-term. That was a new feeling, and it was hard to untangle, but eventually I got there.

Registering for classes the next semester I was stunned to realize that I could study the subject that had suddenly captivated me: women. I enrolled in introductory gender studies courses, and then I dove deep into queer and feminist theory, devouring literature and churning out papers, my mind on fire with ideas. I remember once telling someone what I was studying and she said, "Oh, so you're majoring in lesbianism!" In hindsight the self-obsession of my course load was hilarious. But it was also the first time I felt motivated to do my schoolwork. I was learning not just the history of people I identified with, but also how to *think*. Critical theory was turning my world inside out, and I couldn't get enough. I remember being particularly fascinated, and horrified, by the problems within feminist movements—specifically, the homophobia within the women's rights movement, the racism within lesbian activism, and the transphobia across all of it.

My junior year, I started interning at the Lesbian Herstory Archives, a beautiful old brownstone in Park Slope that's home to the largest collection of archival lesbian materials in the world. Among rare books, file cabinets of old love letters, dusty combat boots, and carefully preserved protest signs, I felt connected to the ghosts of queer women past, and also made a bunch of new friends, many of whom are still among my closest. When I moved to Brooklyn seven years later, I chose an apartment solely because of its proximity to my friend Mimi, an archivist I'd met when I shadowed her during that internship. Being gay opened up a whole new world beyond what I was studying; for the first time in my life, I was part of a community.

And suddenly I was also dating. A lot. With my short hair, I was very visible to other queer women, which helped. I realized the qualities that had made me feel awkward for my whole life—my low, quiet voice, tendency to blush, and the way I always preferred listening over speaking—were actually kind of endearing to other women. Even though my confidence had been so fragile just a few years prior, for the first time in my life, I felt sexually powerful. Numbers were exchanged on the street, on the subway, in classes, at parties, in dark bars that we snuck into. My crushes were boundless. I was flirting with everyone, making out with just about any girl who paid attention to me. But I also felt unsure how to say no to women I wasn't attracted to; it was impossible to set boundaries because I was so unused to being desired in that way. A lot of the women who came on to me said they were straight, which at first felt like a fun challenge and then quickly got old; I was sick of feeling like someone's experiment, especially when claiming my own identity was so new and so important.

At a certain point I suddenly, out of nowhere, fell for a close friend. I had never thought of her as anything other than a pal, but then one day sitting next to each other at some show I was suddenly aware of the warmth from her arm pressing into mine, and my whole body flushed. It was a familiar feeling; I was used to accidentally crushing on friends. Just a few years before, I would have shoved those feelings down. But I was gay now, and so was she, so I went for it. The attraction was mutual, and she spent the night. In the morning, though, she did something that shocked me: she made me promise not to tell anyone. She claimed she didn't want to cause drama in our friend group. She did, however, want to keep sleeping with me. My feelings were really hurt, and I couldn't understand where she was coming from.

To me it was a simple equation: good friends + good sex = great relationship. But she didn't want that and I was under some sort of spell, so we hooked up in secret for months while she dated other girls, bringing them around in front of me but then following me home when they left. I felt raw all the time. Finally, one night over Facebook Messenger she asked if she could come over, and I said no. I knew she'd never want what I wanted, and continuing to see each other in secret was only stretching out my humiliation. Enough was enough. And in saying no, I finally gave myself permission to participate in my own dating life, rather than passively going along with whatever came my way.

So, I joined OkCupid to try to meet girls who were (a) actually gay and (b) actually wanted a relationship. I ended up with a string of much older girlfriends, most of whom treated me like a pet (which was just fine with me—I loved being the object of female affection, so much so that I could overlook how conde-scending it was).

Meanwhile, in school, I wound up in a small class called Feminist Oral History taught by Bettina Aptheker, a visiting professor and well-known feminist and political activist. For my final project I wrote a long-form poem documenting a pattern I had noticed: that all of the queer women I'd dated—which by then was quite a few—had experienced some sort of trauma, and that trauma echoed into their romantic relationships, in-forming their ability to love and trust. Keeping to the oral his-tory form, I used bits of anecdotes they'd told me about the vi-olence they'd experienced, combined with my own experiences of trying to love them while they pushed me away.

The poem was bad. It was definitely at the very least pain-fully cheesy. But when I finished reading it, my classmates had tears in their eyes (at that age we were all, I suppose, prone to overwrought emotions). The real validation came from Jona-than Ned Katz, a famous gay historian, who was auditing the class. After that final presentation, he followed me out and said, "What are you going to do about the fact that you're a writer?"

I blushed and said, "Thank you," and he said, "No, I'm ask-ing you a question. What are you going to do to make sure you can keep writing?"

I wasn't sure. I'd always loved writing but had absolutely no idea how to make it into a career, or even what I wanted to write about besides my own love life. So I started taking journalism classes, and creative writing workshops, and courses about poetry and activism. I did an independent study with a professor I loved about lesbian poetry. I interned at *amNewYork*, a free daily paper, and wrote a little column on music. The next semester, I interned at the Feminist Press, learning how to copy edit, and filling my brain up with dreams of being an author. It was, again, another situation where I'd make lifelong friends.

A friend at the Lesbian Herstory Archives helped me get a job at the feminist, sex-positive sex toy store Babeland. There was a lot of overlap between the staffs at those two places in those days; most dykes I met either worked at one or both, or had a partner who did. Largely inspired by social justice language, the training to be a sex educator at Babeland involved a week of workshops regarding body parts, pronouns, consent, and boundaries. Mostly the job was talking to nervous young people about their first vibrator and explaining different types of lube.

Through this same crowd of people, I also got involved with the New York City Dyke March, and I learned about community organizing. I was trained to be a protest marshal, learning how to keep protestors safe and what to do if someone got arrested. For years, I designed the posters for the march and painted the banners. One year at the Dyke March the cops showed up on scooters, driving so aggressively close to the marchers that they were hitting into their legs, so we held hands and formed a human shield between us and them. Another year while we were holding hands to block off traffic, an angry cop instructed a vehicle to drive right through us, and we held hands until the very last second, the car hitting our arms as it zoomed through. I was surprised to find that when it came to protecting women from men, I could be brave (and maybe a little stupid). Between my job, internship, volunteer work, and group of wonderful queer friends, I felt as though I had found my personal heaven. A decade later, when people would ask me about my background, it was this period of time that I pictured: surrounded by asymmetrical haircuts and all kinds of beautiful bodies, sleeping with each other and gossiping about it, organizing protest actions, caravaning to Riis Beach every weekend before social media made it too crowded to enjoy, rallying around the idea that what made us different and vulnerable could also make us, maybe, cool.

I graduated in 2011, on the heels of the Great Recession. I dreamed of working at a prestigious newspaper, but based on the economy and what was happening in media, there was truly no reason why I should have been able to get a journalism job upon graduating. I had gotten lucky, though. One of the Feminist Press authors was a millionaire who'd made her money running abortion clinics. I'd helped copy edit her memoir and when I was graduating, she needed an assistant to help her with the feminist journal that was published out of one of her health centers in Queens. My intern supervisor recommended me and after an extremely brief, extremely stressful interview with the author herself, the job was mine. It turned out to be a combination of very basic editorial work for the journal and marketing work for the health center. There was one other editor on staff, who worked remotely; I liked her a lot but we rarely saw each other in person. I got to write a few articles, covering things like sex trafficking and abortion rights. My office, in fact, was in the basement of the abortion clinic. I was bored most of the time and so stressed out the rest of the time that I got an ulcer. My boss was prone to yelling at her employees, and while her aggression was rarely directed at me, I lived in fear of the moment it might be.

I was, as far as I could tell, the only lesbian who worked there. One would think that a women's health center would be a safe haven for queer women, but eventually I learned just how wrong that assumption was. One day I overheard a group of my coworkers outside my office talking about a trans woman who had sought care without first notifying the practitioner that she was trans; the nurse discovered it when she went to give her a gynecological exam. Horrified and repulsed by what she saw, the nurse refused to treat her—and then bragged to her coworkers about it, in earshot of me.

I took my complaints up the management chain to the big boss, who agreed that it was unacceptable and let me hire someone to hold sensitivity trainings. I brought in a friend from Babeland who had gone on to work at a health center for queer teenagers, and together we led small teams of people through very basic exercises. Most people had no problem with it. But a few said things like, "I don't care what someone does in their personal life; I just don't want to know about it." From a healthcare professional, that was jarring to hear. It was wild to suddenly know which of my otherwise friendly coworkers were actually transphobic and homophobic.

I gave it exactly one year total, and then I quit. I couldn't stand the pressure of being the sole person fighting for change. Plus, I really didn't see a future for myself there; there was so little work to be done that it was hard to picture what growth might look like, and no one discussed anything of the sort with me. I also was assuming I could easily find another assistant job.

That was wildly naive. I could not get another full-time job. I was newly twenty-three, and I had one year of professional experience, while the rest of my work history wasn't exactly resume appropriate (2010–2011: slinging dildos at Babeland). With nothing left to lose, and money running out, I started pitching editors my writing. Someone who wanted to hire me to write for a gay news website but didn't end up having the budget had put me in touch with the editor of AfterEllen (a lesbian gossip website that, at that point, was still pretty great—years later it would change owners and become a hotbed of transphobia). The first story I ever got paid to write as a freelancer was a recap of the soapy vampire television show *True Blood* for them. My recap style (which reflected my honest love/hate feelings about the show) went over well with the readers, so they asked me to start doing it every week. I'd watch the episode on HBO a couple of times and then stay up all night writing the recap, turning it in by dawn, and then sleeping until noon. After all, I had nowhere to be.

Eventually *Autostraddle*, the world's largest online publishing platform for queer women, put out an open call for contributing editors, and I breathlessly applied. I *loved Autostraddle*. The writing was always interesting, and the people running it were smart and hot—maybe also, at the time, cliquey, but in an aspirational way. I desperately wanted to be part of it, and one of them. I applied with a reported story about the history of a 1973 poster I'd found at the Lesbian Herstory Archives. It was an image of two women, one topless, with the caption I'LL ALWAYS LOVE MY MAMA. I'd left it out on the table at the archives where it was spotted by someone who'd been friends with one of the women in the poster. I was put in touch with her and dug up the whole story, turning it into an essay about visibility across time. I wrote it like a reported feature, but it was extremely emotionally charged, and I felt so excited at the idea that maybe I would get to write more stories like it. When I hit Send, I had goose bumps.

A few weeks later, I got an email saying that I, and a dozen others, had gotten the gig. It was unpaid, with the promise that maybe soon they'd have money. I remember flushing with pride at my laptop. Because it was a remote office, everything happened through email, and I became glued to my screen (and subsequently, my couch). We rotated days of the week to cover breaking news and were encouraged to write columns. Eventually I developed one about queer style called How to Own It, which evolved into a work-focused fashion column called Lez Get Dressed for Work, finding my footing by writing in a service-driven way.

To supplement my income, I got another freelance gig helping a filmmaker do PR for a documentary about women's sex lives. I bounced between writing jobs with that as my main source of income for about a year, until I started interviewing for a production assistant job at Refinery29 that a friend from college had told me about. I finally had more than a couple of things to put on my resume, so I felt like I had a chance. I was also exhausted from cobbling together an income, and I craved the security of a regular paycheck. I had become somewhat of a couch potato, staying inside for weeks at a time if work didn't require me to go anywhere. The rare times that I was required to venture out, I'd get very dressed up. When I told the filmmaker I was applying for that job, I explained, "I secretly love fashion." She laughed, gesturing at my outfit, and said, "It's not a secret."

After my initial phone call with HR, I was asked to come to the office and meet with the beauty director, a woman named Annie Tomlin. I was terrified for my interview, but my fears were unfounded: to my pleasant surprise, Annie, who rounded the corner of desks grinning, with long blonde hair, oversize glasses, and a bright-red jumpsuit, put me at ease immediately. And most surprising of all, one of the first things she said to me was that she loved my writing from *Autostraddle*. We talked about the problem women's media had with queer representation. I said, "I mean, magazines pretend lesbians don't exist." She clapped her hands and said, "Exactly." At the end of the interview she said, "I love you," and I laughed, delighted, saying, "I love you, too." I got the job.

Annie was an incredible boss, as was Megan McIntyre, who was the senior beauty editor. There was also an associate beauty editor named Tara Rasmus, and she quickly became my work wife, giddily Gchatting with me all day while we giggled and gossiped and complained. They encouraged me to write, and they let me follow my heart in terms of what I wanted to write about, which tended to be stories on identity through a beauty lens.

I was the only out lesbian on the editorial staff that I was aware of. Everyone, though, was interested in improving the diversity of the content—they just weren't sure how to do it. I suddenly found myself constantly on the receiving end of questions from people in other verticals about pronouns, and recommendations for queer sources for their stories. I was, as I was told, somehow the only lesbian that many of them even knew, which meant I was their gateway to the entire community. At first I was glad they were asking me for help rather than getting it wrong, but eventually it became a burden. Finally Megan stepped in and spoke to the other managers about clarifying to their teams that my job was to be a beauty assistant, not the token gay girl or the local fountain of queer wisdom (my words, not hers).

For my late teens and early twenties, I had mostly stopped wearing makeup, even though I'd always been kind of a fairy princess at heart. But with an infinite beauty closet to play in, I became reacquainted with that part of myself. Eventually I started growing out my hair and wearing lipstick. Suddenly, for the first time since I came out, I was no longer visibly queer— since feminine queerness is not generally legible to the untrained eye. I was shocked to be constantly faced with the choice of whether or not to come out to people; and I was meeting new people almost every day, thanks to the constant industry events I had to attend.

Usually it went something like this: "Men, *am I right?*"

I'd just sat down at a table toward the back of what was probably the most elegant space I'd ever been in, up a flight of stairs at the Bowery Hotel, to celebrate a perfume or concealer or skin-care miracle—I can't remember. The woman speaking to me had long blonde hair, which was expertly waved, shiny red lipstick, and a tan not consistent with the season; she was laughing with someone else at the table and generously turned to include me in the conversation, which was, I assume, about their boyfriends or their husbands. *Men, amiright?*

"The worst," I replied, with a nervous smile.

It would be weird to say, "Well, actually I'm gay," .02 seconds into meeting someone, but in hindsight I wonder if it's any weirder than the assumption that I wasn't. But I didn't know a single person there and no one hates men more than straight women, and bonding about that is the best way to make new friends when you don't know anyone, and I was more than happy to hear about what this woman's boyfriend/husband did or, more likely, didn't do.

A few minutes later I'd probably find a way to say something about "my girlfriend," or even start a sentence with "as a lesbian" and watch them react. In those situations, straight women were generally *much* nicer to me once they found out I was gay—this was before a lot of other editors pivoted to queerness and I was definitely an anomaly. The niceness could be interpreted in many different ways. Or maybe I wouldn't say anything at all, making friends with them, and then they'd add me on Instagram, seeing an account full of pictures of me being fully gay. Did they care? I don't know. Sometimes. The changes in the way someone treats you once you're out are subtle, unless you're on the receiving end.

Being a lesbian beauty editor in 2013 was isolating. I felt like I constantly had to explain myself, justifying my own presence. Discourse around beauty as self-care, as something you did for yourself and not for a man, had yet to really take hold. I was constantly surrounded by discussions of which red lipstick men like best. And conversely it was tough to explain my work to my activist friends, especially the older ones, who had devoted their lives to making the world better—and there I was, making lipstick swabs on my hands all day. I knew how it sounded. But I also got a thrill out of making the beauty space queerer, and commenters were responding gratefully. It wasn't exactly activism, but it was a small difference I could easily make.

After working at Refinery for almost a year, I got an email from someone in another vertical saying that he wanted to do a story (from the perspective of a woman) loosely titled "Gay Men We Wish Were Straight." In order to achieve balance, he asked me to write a counter story, loosely titled, "Straight Women We Wish Were Gay." He had cc'd his editor, and she too was on board with this request. I got the email on a Saturday morning. I was stunned at the ignorance. I responded back looping in Annie, explaining why it was problematic to write about wishing someone identified differently just to suit your own desires—it was, I wrote, akin to saying someone was "a waste" for being gay. Annie took me out for coffee later that day to process it, and I felt grateful to have a manager who was on the same page, while deeply disturbed by how little some of my much older colleagues—who were by all means progressive and empathetic—understood about how to talk to and about queer people.

After some more conversations with other senior editors, I decided to take it upon myself to improve the way the editorial staff approached the topic of LGBTQ people by writing an addendum to the style guide. I called it "The Primer for Radical Inclusivity" and, using a lot of things I'd learned in college and at Babeland, went on to outline ways to write respectfully about queer people. I submitted it to the executive editor, who implemented it and told me it had inspired her to create a similar one for talking about race. ("Radical inclusivity" became a core value of Refinery, though those words were used in 2020 to illustrate what many identified as the company's hypocrisy when it was called out by former and current employees for institutionalized racism.)

When I left Refinery29 for *Nylon*, I looked very different, even though barely two years had passed. I'd started working there with an asymmetrical pixie cut, my hair thick and shiny in its natural, undyed state, and I wore very little makeup every day: just some black liquid liner and mascara. I dressed in button-ups tucked into pants. By the time I quit, my hair was long and bleached pink-blonde, and I was wearing dresses and lipstick. I wore a knee-length black T-shirt dress to my first day at *Nylon*, thinking it was edgy but quickly realizing that, compared to my new coworkers, it was extremely boring, bordering on preppy.

Because *Nylon* was already a pretty queer brand, I didn't go on the same campaign for change that I did at Refinery, which meant that not everyone knew I was a lesbian until getting to know me. One girl on the publishing side said something to me along the lines of, "You know, I thought you were some J. Crew bitch until I realized that you're gay, which makes you cool." I took the compliment, even with the barbs. It's funny to imagine myself as some J. Crew bitch—me, who on the inside will always feel like a weird art girl with purple hair and acne, making up love songs on my guitar for my best friend and recording them on an 8-track in my bedroom. But I guess we never really know how other people see us.

When I went on press trips, though, it was always a burden to have to decide when and where and how to come out in these new groups of adults in faraway places, while the writers and editors chatted around me about their husbands. I never went on a press trip with another lesbian. Usually I tried to get it out of the way immediately, and absolutely always at some point no matter what the trip was or where we were, another woman, usually older, would get drunk, pull me aside conspiratorially, and tell me secrets. I heard a lot of fun stories this way. In the hills of Northern Italy, for example, after many courses of homemade pizza and several glasses of wine, one publicist whispered to me about the time she fucked a very famous female rock star.

It wasn't always fun stories, though. Sometimes it was uncomfortable questions like, But haven't you ever wanted to be with a man? Or, Have you ever had a boyfriend and what did he look like? Is it really better between women? Do you like *pretty* girls? All the people who asked me these questions thought that because they clarified that they were politically progressive, it wasn't offensive.

Sometimes it was blatantly offensive. In a hot tub in Mexico a woman told me my armpit hair was disgusting. On a trip to Cuzco, Peru, I asked our tour guide if the rainbow flags around the city were for gay pride, and a shadow passed over his face as he explained that it was the flag of the city, and when it comes to gay people, "We don't have those here."

Today, there are so many more editors who identify as queer than when I was starting out. I love seeing people I've known for years update their Instagram bio with a little rainbow, or shoot out a declaratively queer tweet. I think of all the people who stopped talking to me in 2008 because I had a girlfriend, and I wonder what they think of the wave of queerness that has taken hold. Maybe they are part of it. I wouldn't know; I have kind of a scorched-earth policy for people who have wronged me and don't care to keep track of them even virtually.

Someone recently asked me if I've always been out at work, and I didn't know how to answer, because my work has always been tied to my lesbian identity. It's what got me writing in the first place, and it informs almost everything I do. When I became editor in chief, straight people in media constantly wanted to try to tell me that it didn't matter that I was gay, that we were living in some sort of golden age for queer people where your value is determined by the quality of your work, not who you are. I could see how they might have thought that based on the sheer number of people who now identify as queer— according to a report by J. Walter Thompson Innovation Group in 2016, only 48 percent of Gen Z in the US identified as exclusively heterosexual. But with no other lesbians at the tippy top of major fashion mastheads, I couldn't help but feel like it did matter, maybe more than ever. Young queer women still tell me things like they didn't think it was possible for a lesbian to be an editor in chief until they heard about me. The fact that we live in a world where I can scream from the rooftops about how gay I am doesn't mean the work is over. It means it can finally begin in earnest.

3

Aren't You
a Little Young?

When she was twenty-eight, my mom married my dad.

For me and my two sisters, twenty-eight became a golden number. Young enough to be fresh faced and glowing—as my mom is in her wedding photos, with short, elegant light-brown hair and a glamorous, thin frame—but old enough to use proper judgment when deciding who to spend the rest of your life with. Case in point: my parents are still happily married.

When we were twenty-eight, my twin sister got married. I did her makeup, but she hardly needed any her skin was so radiant with joy. She was the only one of us to match my mom's marriage timeline, which we had all idealized.

Marrying someone, though, couldn't have been further from my mind. In my twenty-eighth year of life, I was married to my job. That was the year I became editor in chief.

To my surprise, the hardest part of getting that title was having to tell people. And I had a lot of telling to do. There was no major announcement around the promotion—no chic cocktail party with designers and actresses to celebrate my success. The news that day, and the weeks that followed, was that the magazine had been folded.

So, I hit the ground running on my own DIY word-of-mouth self-promotion campaign. It was, in many ways, totally embarrassing to have to tell people that I'd reached the top of the masthead at a major publication, as most people who step into that kind of position generate a ton of press for doing so. There was also the fact of my age—and, worse, my baby face. I hardly looked the too-young-for-the-job age that I was. I practiced it in the mirror: "Hi, I'm Gabrielle Korn. I'm the editor in chief of *Nylon*." I thought it sounded dubious even to my own reflection.

I quickly learned the difference between people who were happy for me and people who thought I didn't deserve the title by their response to the news. An eyes-wide "Wow!" was not good; a hand on a heart with an "oh my god" was great. And in general, I stopped telling strangers altogether: being in your twenties and saying, "I'm the EIC of a women's media company" to someone outside the industry whose only references are Anna Wintour and Miranda Priestly usually caused people to express disbelief. If they hadn't heard of *Nylon*, they assumed it was something I maybe started in my dorm room.

If someone was much older than me, they almost always said, "Aren't you a little young?" My responses ranged from "Well, I'm almost thirty" to "I guess I must be good at it." But defensiveness and sassiness are exhausting, so eventually I stopped giving details to new people at all, resorting to just telling them vaguely that I was an editor at a magazine.

I felt conflicted about my new role. On the one hand I was enormously proud of myself; it was a huge deal to be the editor in chief, and I was thrilled at the thought that I'd finally be entitled to make the changes I wanted to make. But on the other hand I was terrified and felt like a total imposter. I knew that other women had worked decades before getting a role like mine, and I'd skipped many steps. Despite my outward defensiveness, I knew I was more than just "a little young" for the job.

But really, according to the feedback I got from the world at large, I'd been too young for every single step of my career except when I was an assistant in my early twenties. As soon as I got an editor title I was met with raised eyebrows from peers and people older than me. I don't think that men face this challenge; what I've observed is that men in my industry who get ahead early are called trailblazers, while women who get ahead early are simply not taken seriously. The messaging is confusing:

we're repeatedly told we should want to look young. Our culture is, in fact, obsessed with it; the global antiaging industry
was valued at 250 *billion* dollars in 2016 and has grown year over
year ever since. But if we do look young, and furthermore if
we *are* young, we're treated like we don't know anything. For a
culture that is so preoccupied with maintaining female youth,
we certainly have quite a few parameters around what kind of
power that youth is allowed to access.

Within that catch-22 was the issue of compensation. In the
women's digital media boom of the 2010s, writers and editors
were not paid a lot, even while we worked for companies that
experienced commercial success. I was thrown into luxurious
situations that I never would have been able to afford on my
salary—press trips around the world, exclusive spa visits, res-
ervations at the nicest restaurants in the city, even haircuts by
celebrity stylists. And I was propped up in front of cameras,
hosting videos and sometimes attempting to model. I frequently
borrowed clothing in order to fake the appearance of being expensive, and in order to convey the message that I belonged.

I was surrounded by other women in their early twenties
who were feeling the effects of that disconnect; the way we
were paid so little yet treated to so much. Many of us were told
that our youth was the reason why we weren't paid more, while
at the same time that youth was clearly what got us attention.

To me, it seemed like the model was to hire young, ambitious women, work them as hard as possible for as little money

as possible until they burn out, and then replace them with a younger, cheaper person from the metaphorical line of people waiting for the chance to have a byline in a beloved publication. I was terrified of burning out and being replaced. I feared that one day I would wake up and simply not have any more ideas, and that would be the end of my career.

At the same time, I was amazed that I was even making money as a writer at all. Like many entry-level writers, I was hired at Refinery29 with a salary of $40K. It was exactly the amount I had asked for, and I was thrilled with it. I'd been trying to make it in digital media for two years—the first year as an editorial assistant at *On The Issues Magazine* ($15/hour), and the second as a freelance writer taking whatever gig I could get my hands on, which included recapping *True Blood* ($30/article), writing marketing materials for a documentary about women's sex lives ($15/hour), and eventually the fashion column at *Autostraddle* (a one-time bonus of $500), which got me noticed by Refinery.

That first year as a beauty assistant, my writing was responsible for bringing in a solid chunk of traffic to our vertical. (I knew this because we had complete transparency into the numbers through production reports that tracked exactly how we were doing.) Plus, because I was so vocal about how we needed to be more inclusive of queer people, I had very tangibly shaped the direction of the content. I looked forward to getting a promotion. But a year in, when it came time for promotions and raises, my title was changed from beauty assistant to assistant beauty editor, and I was given a raise of one thousand dollars. I didn't think my new title was fair—in my mind, it wasn't even really an upgrade, just a word switch—and the raise was actually less than a cost-of-living increase would have been. I protested up the chain of command until my complaints reached the editor in chief, who agreed to raise my salary to $45K and gave me the title of associate beauty editor.

I was grateful, but not satisfied. Thanks to our regular champagne toasts when the company landed million-dollar deals, I knew there was money around, and I felt like I was being taken advantage of. I (clearly) didn't understand how profit margins worked but I thought it seemed ridiculous that editors and writers weren't compensated proportionally to their contributions. I was sick of working in such a glamorous environment without a glamorous paycheck to match it. But the final straw was that after I fought for that extra $5K, two people who both had less experience than me were added to my department in roles senior to mine. It felt like a slap in the face. I complained to management and was told my Instagram following wasn't big enough to consider me for a senior role. They were investing in "industry stars." I wasn't one.

I also didn't understand that to get significantly more money, you usually have to get a new job. But that ignorance served me; if I'd had a better understanding of how it all worked, I wouldn't have fought so hard for myself. As Elaine Welteroth wrote in her memoir about her own professional trajectory,

"PLEASE NOTE THE ABSOLUTE INSANE AUDACITY OF A MILLENNIAL IN HER TWENTIES."

I am truly astounded by this younger version of me. But like, get it, girl.

Because my byline was out there, it was easy to hit the job interview circuit, and I met with editors until I got an offer for $55K from *Us Weekly* for a staff writing position. I wasn't really excited about the opportunity, so I used the offer as leverage to get a matching offer from Refinery, and my title was changed to beauty editor. Word spread quickly about how difficult and demanding I'd been, but it had been worth it. I was thrilled with the amount—it sounded like *so much money*!

As I quickly realized, though, I didn't love the job enough to stay indefinitely for any amount. I was suddenly really sick of beauty—I wasn't someone who got excited about new products or followed the lives of models, and it's exhausting to only approach a topic as something to be dismantled. I was burned out, and the additional money didn't make the difference I thought it would.

So when I got an email from Michelle Lee, the editor in chief of *Nylon*, saying she was building out her digital team, I almost instantly knew that I'd be taking the job if she offered it. I still remember what her email looked like on the screen, short and to the point. We met at a sun-drenched restaurant in Soho, and over sashimi and lattes she told me about her vision for *Nylon*. I wore a black-and-white-striped top with black pleather pants. She had a leather jacket draped chicly over her shoulders, her elbows on the table as she excitedly told me about working at this small indie magazine that I'd loved since I was a teenager. I found her totally charming and I was interested in her ideas; she knew in order to survive, the magazine needed a strong digital presence, so she was going after digitally native editors with proven track records. Plus she, like me, was interested in trying to fix media's diversity problem, and she listened intently while I blabbered on about queer representation in the beauty space. My age didn't come up once in the conversation. Within a few weeks I completed an edit test and she offered me the job over email. It all happened so quickly and easily it felt dreamlike. It was a senior editor position for $68K, and I knew Refinery wouldn't try to match it—they'd matched the *Us Weekly* offer only months before.

In fighting to get more money, I had become a total pain in the ass. But I don't think there would have been any other way to do it. My editors were shocked when I quit, especially since I had just gotten not one but two raises. (Years later, one of my star employees quit shortly after I fought to get her a big raise, and I was painfully reminded of my own behavior. That said, I wouldn't change a thing.)

Eventually, though, the women who'd been my biggest cheerleaders were thrilled for me, especially when I explained that the role would be overseeing all the digital verticals, not just beauty, and that I'd get four pages in the magazine to call my own. It was October 2014. I was twenty-five and a half.

Admittedly, *Nylon* was an option I had never considered before. I wasn't sure what to make of it. Historically, like many other magazines, it had a huge diversity problem. Founded in 1999, all the cover stars were white until 2003's Lil' Kim cover; they continued to be white until 2007's Nicole Richie cover, and then stayed white until Zoe Saldana's cover in 2010. That's three women of color in eleven years. The pattern continued of having one woman of color every few years, with all of the other cover stars being white and thin. By 2013, the last year *Nylon* was still being run by its original founders, not much had changed; the cover stars were all white except for Selena Gomez, who is half-Mexican. Then, the magazine was sold and new leadership came in, following a massive round of layoffs. Racial diversity improved over the next couple of years under Michelle's leadership, and I trusted that her interest in me meant I could help with that shift.

About a month before I started, Leila Brillson had been hired to be *Nylon*'s digital director. She too had come from Refinery29, from the entertainment department. Leila was an unconventional-looking boss—with tattoos and ripped fishnets, she rejected any sort of normative idea about what a professional woman should look like, and I really looked up to her. She was a self-proclaimed weird girl who quickly became one of my closest friends, despite also being my direct manager.

Following the layoffs, there were two remaining junior

digital editors, and they were less than thrilled to suddenly have new bosses. On my first day, when Leila introduced me to them, they wouldn't even look up from their computers to say hi. It was like being in middle school all over again. They made me feel so worthless that I called my mom that night crying, wondering if I'd made a huge mistake.

Rather than wallow, though, I spent the next few months making a point to take my new coworkers out to lunch, willing them to like me. Leila was in her thirties with a lot more professional experience than me, and I realized immediately that if I was ever going to be seen as something other than her little pal, I needed to keep my age a secret from the editors. It worked; I was told my colleagues assumed I was over thirty, too. Eventually I found myself being a trusted confidante for many of them, a kind of pseudo-HR in place of an actual human resources department, a go-to adult. I was also assigning, editing, and writing stories, maintaining the editorial calendar, helping with social media, and working closely with the video department. In many ways, the person who is second in command always does the actual job of a director; while Leila was in big-picture meetings with other executives, I was in the trenches, and most of the time it felt like I was holding up the department with my bare hands.

I was largely making things up as I went, but it was working; my instincts for what made good content was resonating with our readers, and I seemed to be pretty good at managing people—processes were becoming streamlined under me and I loved watching younger writers and editors come into their own with my guidance. After a year, Leila promoted me to deputy editor and gave me a nice raise. It was the first time in my life I'd gotten a raise without fighting for one.

A few months later, quite suddenly, half the print team was let go.

Within a few months of that round of layoffs, in 2015, Michelle left for *Allure*, and in what became a year of rapid structural change, eventually we got a new CEO, and then Leila abruptly left, too, which meant the digital department was left without an official leader.

My new boss called me into his office and said, "Can you do her job, or do I need to hire someone else?" I looked him straight in the eyes and said, "I'm already doing it." He changed my title to digital director and gave me a small raise, promising to revisit it in six months depending on how successful I was. I was about to turn twenty-seven.

Because of her entertainment background, Leila had been very good at driving clicks with news, and it made our traffic grow quickly. That was great for our bottom line, but I felt like we were getting away from what I loved the most about *Nylon*, which was quality feature stories on emerging culture and beautiful original photography that had a very recognizable aesthetic. I also personally just wasn't interested in having to keep up with celebrity gossip. By the time she left I had a running mental list of everything I wanted to do differently, and so, given the keys to the kingdom, I poured myself into re-strategizing. At weekly manager meetings, I'd come with pages and pages of typed notes documenting all of the changes I was making and what the results were; it made my boss happy but resulted in a lot of side-eye from the other department heads.

In those meetings, as the youngest person in the room, I felt that I had a lot to prove. I needed to convince them that I understood how the internet worked while having a thorough knowledge of what quality journalism looks like, plus a mastery of the brand and superior management skills. It was "fake it until you make it" on crack, because I technically *had* made it but still needed to fake it in a lot of ways. With Leila gone, there was no one to mentor me anymore—the new CEO wasn't from an editorial background, so I was pretty much on my own.

As it turns out, though, I knew a lot more than I thought I did. I was positively thriving from being in charge of digital. I hired a bunch of really smart people, a few with more experience than me. I wanted our site to reflect my own political beliefs, because I knew that our new younger readers, like me, cared about issues of race, feminism, and queerness, while also being deeply invested in beauty, fashion, and music, so I put marginalized voices and their stories front and center.

Politics was new territory for the brand. It wasn't something that was addressed directly in print; though they'd talk about feminism and girl power, there was little to no discussion of actual politics, nor even politicized intimacy. I tried again and again to convince the print editors to cover sex and relationships, and it was a dead end. One editor in particular who always openly hated me for no discernible reason said, after I proposed adding sex content to their pages, "We're never going to write 'how to please your man' stories," and then scoffed in my face. I replied something along the lines of, "Do you really think that's what I'm suggesting? Can you really not imagine sex content not centered around male pleasure?" But she won the argument; I had no control over the magazine. We did it online, though, and it was very successful.

I wanted to be as progressive as possible, which often resulted in tension with my boss. Certain advertisers didn't want to be aligned with certain content, like one essay in particular that I wrote about trying out marijuana suppositories for my cramps. But there was no point to me working that hard, I told myself, if I wasn't going to try to make the world a better place in the process, through stories that served and reflected a diverse readership.

And when it came time for that six-month review I was promised, it was stellar; my strategy had worked, and we were not only growing but gaining respect in the industry. My title was subsequently changed from digital director to digital editor in chief, and I was given another raise, which brought my salary to six figures. It sounded like the most money in the world.

But it quickly became clear that, even though the company

strategy was tilting toward digital, the industry at large only recognized the value of an editor-in-chief title—the digital qualifier in mine meant that I came second to the person running the magazine. Print carried a level of prestige that digital simply didn't. The editor in chief sat front row at Fashion Week while I sat behind her, watching the shows over her shoulder as I tried to take iPhone photos for Instagram. I was desperate for her approval, or at least some mentorship, since she was so much more experienced than me and very smart, but I was growing tired of the industry treating me like my work didn't matter. It all felt very backward based on how the readers were actually finding us.

Eventually, our boss decided that he wanted me to be above her. He suggested the title chief content officer, but I didn't want it because I worried about peaking too early; where would I, at twenty-seven, go from there? We tossed words around until we landed on global editor in chief, and I agreed to be the liaison between all of our international editions. It was a huge promotion. But while my digital team was delighted for me, the print team was pretty furious; my boss told me that one of their editors had even made a concerted effort to challenge my promotion, holding meetings in which she allegedly presented my age and my personal social media presence as reasons among many that I was unfit for the title. That weekend was gay pride in NYC, and in response to hearing she'd taken issue with my Instagram, I posted a photo of my butt on the beach. It was definitely petty, and maybe proved her point, but it was also cathartic and, in hindsight, hilarious.

There was one major problem with my new promotion, aside from the internal issues: I didn't get a raise. As I'd come to find out, my salary was, in fact, less than that of one of my junior colleagues in a different department. My current salary was totally fucking amazing for what my experience level was, but ridiculous for a global title and my actual responsibilities, and completely unfair (bordering on illegal) compared to what my straight white male coworker was making to do a less senior job.

I wasn't sure what to do. I had gotten a raise just a few months prior, but this was a real promotion, with a lot of added responsibilities, and I felt like I was being taken advantage of because I was a young woman. I began reaching out to friends in the industry for advice. Finally I spoke with someone who estimated that, as a global editor in chief of such an internationally respected brand, I should be making at least two hundred thousand dollars—basically twice my salary. But I had no idea how to go about asking for that kind of money, and it weighed on me heavily. One day I ran into a woman from accounting in the bathroom and I mentioned my new global title to her. She said she hadn't been told about it. She asked me if I was going to ask for a raise, and I told her that I had, unsuccessfully. She asked me how much money I wanted. I said I didn't know for sure, but I'd been told that someone with my title should be making at least twice what I was.

That night I got an email from my boss that said we needed

to speak as soon as I got to the office. I was up all night worrying, so I went in super early and waited for him. As it turned out, the woman I'd spoken to in the bathroom had told him about our conversation, but had abbreviated it—she had told him that I was about to ask for my salary to be doubled, without any context. She was in his office when I went in, but we didn't look at each other (in fact, we never spoke again). My boss's face was red, and there was a vein I'd never seen before lit up across his forehead; his knees were bouncing aggressively under his desk, hands opening and closing rapidly. He told me that if I wanted that kind of money I should work elsewhere. I protested that I hadn't actually been asking for that amount, that I was simply telling someone in a casual conversation about advice I had been given. He didn't seem to hear me and yelled at me for nearly half an hour about how I was entitled and ungrateful; he'd given me a huge opportunity, he said, and I was just using my title as leverage, and what did I even need that kind of salary at my age for?

I said that I loved my job and I was happy to do it, but I didn't know if I could continue pouring my whole self into it without being compensated fairly.

He said, "If that's the case, this isn't the job for you."

I got up and left, shaking so much that I accidentally slammed his sliding door.

We didn't speak for two weeks. A coworker who was close with him suggested to me that maybe he was hurt that I hadn't come to him directly with the ask. Eventually I realized it was on me to make it right, so I knocked on his door and let myself in. Holding in my pride, I apologized. I said I hadn't meant to disrespect him, and I was grateful for the opportunity. He said he was sorry for overreacting, and that he had just been worried I was about to quit on him, and we agreed to move forward. He said that since it was still the beginning of my career I shouldn't be so concerned with salary because the title was all that mattered. I didn't get any more money, nor did I ask him again.

One of the things my new title meant was that I was supposed to find a way for digital and print to work together, at which I was mostly unsuccessful: the digital team felt that the print team acted superior to them, and the print team felt like the digital team was diluting their brand. Both groups of people expressed to me that they felt left out by the other, but no one was willing to put in the work to be included. There were exactly two people who were willing to help, and those people became hybrid editors, but otherwise we were at a standstill. It was an impossible situation; there was no one enforcing my authority, so people who I didn't manage were free to disregard me. My boss wanted me on camera hosting videos and at fancy events, so in that way my title was useful, but I wasn't overseeing the magazine at all—I wanted to, but that department basically just ignored me. So truthfully I was still just a digital editor in chief who sometimes emailed with people in Korea and Germany about image sizes.

A year went by. And then, suddenly, everything changed.

We all knew *something* was coming because of the company-wide "strategy" meeting that was set to take place in three separate conference rooms. It was September 7, 2017. The email came around eleven a.m. Actually, some of us had realized for weeks that something weird was happening. Strange old white guys in suits had been coming in and out of the *Nylon* office, having closed-door meetings with executives. Our CEO had been gone for a suspicious amount of time. Various people closest to him had been spotted crying in the bathroom and they wouldn't say why.

The print team was sequestered in the main conference room, while my teams, as well as the marketing and sales teams, were told to go to the building's conference room downstairs, which was by the lobby elevators. That was odd—it wasn't part of our office. We waited for what felt like forever until the company's owner and a woman from HR came in, looking exhausted and stressed. The HR person told us that the cost of our health insurance was increasing. We all looked around at each other, as if to say, Was that . . . all we came down here for? Obviously it wasn't, and the owner proceeded to explain what a hard decision it was but that the October issue of *Nylon* magazine would be the last.

There was silence. Finally I said, "What about the print editors?"

He looked surprised by the question, and clarified that

they'd all been laid off, effective immediately. I felt like an idiot for not realizing what that meant, but in truth he hadn't actually said the words. Several people began to cry. Most of them just stared silently.

Eventually he left and we were told that we had to remain in the room until the print editors had cleared out their belongings and left the premises. Meanwhile, the press release announcing the closure had gone out the moment we were told it was happening, and all of our phones had begun blowing up with texts and emails. We sat there for just under two hours.

Later that day, after we'd been released, we got an email asking us to come in to work at eight a.m. on Monday. That was even stranger, perhaps, than the layoffs: we weren't what you'd call a morning group. Plus, it was smack-dab in the middle of Fashion Week, a time when sleep is rare and precious. I tried to protest it to the owner, saying we had been through enough already, but he replied that the news he had to tell us was urgent, and he didn't want us to have to wait any longer. I had truly no clue what the announcement would be. More layoffs? An acquisition? The weekend was a blur. I don't even really remember it; my memory flashes from that conversation to stumbling into the office at 7:45 a.m., puffy and cranky. The news that he had for us was that our CEO had resigned, and once again, we'd be getting a new one.

After a speech about this person's qualifications, he introduced his son.

It is, as I'd soon learn, very common for privately owned media companies to be family businesses. And in a way, in theory, working for a family business is a lot more secure than working for a corporation: they have a personal interest in your success. I was also deeply relieved that our CEO was leaving. Even though he and I had somewhat worked out our conflict, I knew he'd never fully take me seriously as a professional adult, and I craved a fresh start with someone who might have more respect for what I was capable of.

In my first meeting with my new boss, I asked if I could take the word "global" out of my title, and he had no idea what I was talking about. And as it turned out, "global editor in chief" had never been officially entered into any sort of HR system anyway, so the title truly was a joke—*no one* higher up knew about it. I became the editor in chief, period, no qualifier.

Because of the context of my promotion, though, there was no announcement to the press. There wasn't even an internal memo; at our first company-wide meeting post-layoffs, the new organizational chart was presented, and there I was, quietly at the top. It did not feel like a victory.

Several days later, in an Uber to a fashion show, a colleague said to me, "You know, in the made-for-TV movie about *Nylon,* you're not the good guy."

She was the only print editor who hadn't been let go, because she was part-time anyway and also had been there since basically the beginning. I was complaining to her about how stressful it had been to go through so many rounds of layoffs over the years, and she cut me off.

She continued, "You're the young digital person who took the older print woman's job." She was laughing, but it wasn't entirely a joke. And it confirmed my worst fear: that everyone hated me, that I stood for change and not in a good way, and that people would somehow blame me for a beloved magazine's demise. I felt like a cockroach in the apocalypse, outlasting everyone, but not because of merit.

In reality, I had literally no idea it was going to happen. Our former CEO had actually made a point of fighting for print to continue, which was questionable in a time when digital was growing and print wasn't, but either way he had given no indication to me that the magazine was selling poorly enough to warrant a closure.

As the EIC, the *only* EIC, the weight of my role was finally apparent from my title, and I could become the face; my values could be the company values. I needed a real raise, for my own morale, and because being the face of the brand is literally more expensive than just being an editor—in so many ways I was required to look the part, and that was eating up my paychecks faster than I could have imagined.

Our new CEO was exactly the same age as me, so I trusted that my age wouldn't be a factor in the conversation. And honestly it wasn't; when I told him about what had happened between his predecessor and me, he agreed to give me a 12 percent raise, which was less than I'd asked for but more than nothing. I was relieved. It was enough to make a difference in my quality of life, and ultimately it felt really good to not be treated like asking for money meant I was entitled or ungrateful.

In October, the last issue of *Nylon* print came out and featured musician Annie Clark, a thin white woman. As I scrambled to figure out what to keep from the magazine's heritage and what to leave in the past, one thing was certain: there needed to be a major ideological shift in the way content was created.

Now that I was in charge, I could take a step back and look at the big picture of the brand and what it meant in the context of what was happening politically and culturally in the US. I had realized over the past few years that almost every women's lifestyle publication was chasing some idea of coolness, but the people who *I* considered the coolest—the artists, the activists, the DIY musicians—weren't reading them. Despite that, coolness had always been core to the brand's DNA, and now it was up to me to define it for our audience. The more I thought about it, though, the more meaningless the word became. Who the fuck was I to determine coolness? And what was the relevance of the brand if it was attaching the idea of coolness to one specific body and background, and leaving everyone else out? I did not want to limit the scope to people like me; I did not think that my own identity was the pinnacle of coolness. It was something more abstract than that, and it needed to be liberated from class, race, and gender. Because in limiting taste to something that only privileged people could claim, it seemed to me that fashion media had actually made itself nearly irrelevant.

It was a major disconnect, and it wasn't hard to figure out the source. Rather than focusing on diversifying audiences, from a marketing perspective, the brand had been attempting to define the reader as a singular "girl," and conversations around strategy always centered on trying to describe who she was. *Who is the reader?* we were asked, again and again. *Who should she be?*

As a more junior editor, when I protested the validity of the question, I was told that it was standard marketing lingo and not to read too deep into it. But it seemed to me that when the people asking that question are relatively old-school, and they've been creating media for a specific kind of white/thin/straight/rich aspiration, the answer becomes a symbol of their own biases, a self-fulfilling prophecy. Their reader was like them. And many of them don't even realize it's happening, because under patriarchy whiteness is read as a neutral identity, as is heterosexuality and skinniness, and so people were getting away with saying that their reader was this one girl, as though that opened them up to a lot of different possibilities instead of limiting them.

When you can describe your reader as one person and say exactly what she likes and where she spends her money, it's easier to pitch advertisers. But it's not easy to grow an audience that way—not to mention it's literally the definition of institutionalized racism, homophobia, and fatphobia. And I heard *so many stories* from not that long ago about editors in chief across the industry who would frequently say that someone was not "on-brand" if they didn't fit that mold. The language of "on-brand" or "off-brand" became an excuse to uphold oppressive values.

So when I was promoted to editor in chief and it was up to me to ask who the reader was, I decided the problem wasn't finding an answer but the question itself.

After all, I had seen firsthand online how diverse our readership truly was, and upon my promotion and raise I was being told I had to triple traffic within the next year, and I knew limiting the audience to one kind of person would never get us there.

I also quickly realized that the covers—however problematic they had been over the years—were iconic enough that we needed to keep doing them in order to keep the readers happy and engaged. Of the other magazines that had ceased print, not many of them were doing digital covers yet, so the plan was a bit of a gamble. There was no road map. But maybe, just maybe, I didn't want one anyway. The more I pored over previous editorial strategies, the more I realized that there was a problem so enmeshed in the brand's DNA that fixing it would require a top-to-bottom overhaul, starting with that age-old question of who the reader was.

I changed it from "Who is she?" to "Who are they?"—a simple word switch with massive implications: it was a readership, not a reader. And that readership needed to be racially diverse AF, with the whole rainbow of sex and gender identities, with all kinds of bodies and from all types of places. What should unite them is not their demographic profile but their values, which the content could reflect back to them. As for what those values were? Well, they were mine: I wanted to create media that was actively anti-racist, progressively feminist, queer encompassing, interested in sustainability, and aesthetically oriented but only in a way that fit the previous ideas. This opened up a whole new world of emerging culture to cover, united by an underlying progressive vibe while being wildly different in scope.

"They" also represented a gender-neutral future. I killed the men's magazine, *Nylon Guys*, with the goal of transcending gender entirely. There would be no ideal *Nylon* reader. *Nylon* would be a community, a web of communities, a *lifestyle*.

The topics that had performed the best online—politics, wellness, and sex—became core to the new digital strategy, with a brand-new vertical called Life to encompass the stuff our readers cared about the most.

I wanted the people creating the content to be diverse, too, from the editors and writers to the crews on set. That, I felt, was the ultimate way to revolutionize media: from the inside. All-female crews are a given, and within that, I tried to hire as many women of color as possible—especially if the person they were photographing wasn't white. The 2019 February cover star, Aja Naomi King, looked into the camera with tears in her eyes and said that it was the first time she'd been on set where the photographer *and* the stylist/glam team were black women; she put her hands together and said, "Thank you, *Nylon*." Similarly when the cover stars were queer, I tried to create LGBTQ crews, which fostered a sense of community like nothing else. This was the most important part of my job to me, and it's what made the long hours and endlessly fast pace worth it.

All in all, I was able to triple my salary in five years—from when I was hired as an assistant at Refinery to when I became EIC of *Nylon*. Sometimes I wondered if it was worth it, if maybe I should have left *Nylon* before even becoming the digital director and gone to a place where I had more people to learn from, so that I could have slowly climbed a corporate ladder instead of being catapulted to the top of it simply because no one around me knew how to internet better than I did. But at the same time I felt confident in my skills as an editor in chief, and I had nothing but pride for what my team created every day. I don't think there's anything I could have absorbed slowly that would replace what I was able to teach myself and what I learned from hands-on experience. Because I hadn't had formal training, I didn't hesitate to radically change the brand from the inside out.

Something I struggled with a lot was the fact that my six-figure salary was a huge amount of money for my age, and more importantly in the context of middle-class America, but for the average salary of my title and the work I was doing, I was still being underpaid. I was plagued with guilt for wanting more and then also beating myself up for being so spoiled. Surely I should have just been grateful to get a regular paycheck at all in media. My older friends yelled at me when I'd say that out loud. I'm still not sure where the line is.

While I was EIC, an intern came to me for career advice. She was a women's studies major and had heard that I had been, too, and she couldn't get over the fact that I'd studied something so traditionally "useless" and managed to have a career. She also said that she had heard I was "self-made." I honestly had no idea what she meant.

She explained, "That you got this job so young with no one helping you."

I still didn't get it. Who would help me?

She clarified further, "That, like, you're not related to anyone."

I had to hold in a laugh. The thought of a relative helping me in my career was so far-fetched that it didn't even occur to me that people might think otherwise. I had forgotten how many media people who get ahead young are able to do so because a family member puts in a good word with someone close to them. My parents, who both work in healthcare, set me up for success in a lot of ways: they taught me the value of education, of being kind and a good person, of working hard, of taking care of the people you love. They love me a lot and are always there for me. No one in my family, though, connected me to anyone in media for jobs when I was starting out—not because they didn't want to, but simply because we're not a media family. I entered this industry not knowing a single person.

After that interaction, I had a new sense of pride. Sure, a lot of my promotions were purely because I was in the right place at the right time, but every win felt squarely like my own.

After I spent a year as editor in chief, I started generating press. Finally there was a story to tell, and it was a success story. I had reinvented the brand, somewhat of a risk for a fashion magazine, and as a result we were surviving in a time when our competitors were folding. My age was included in almost every headline, if not the first sentence, but it wasn't written in a condescending way anywhere; if anything, there was a sense of admiration and respect. One journalist, for NewNowNext, wrote the following:

> These days, Nylon is going a lot deeper than just young women's fashion, beauty, and glittery pop culture. In fact, a sampling of its latest content includes stories on queer Brazilian films, an upbeat ruling for transgender students in Oregon, and Planned Parenthood's plan to open more locations in the South.
>
> Under the guidance of 29-year-old Gabrielle Korn, an out lesbian who lives in Brooklyn with her musician girlfriend, Nylon has become one of the most politically-aware, racially diverse, LGBTQ-inclusive, and feminist-forward digital magazines out there since Korn was appointed editor-in-chief in September 2017 (the same time the outlet's print edition folded).

My age had become a detail that made my story more compelling, not more suspicious. I *was* a little young for the job but was succeeding anyway.

My absolute least favorite part of being the boss was having to say no to young women who weren't satisfied with their salaries. It was so weird to be on the other end of a money conversation. When I hired people, I made sure to get them the best possible offer I could, but at the end of the day I didn't really control what the budget was. Having insight into budgets and perspective about age and ability gave me a newfound empathy for the people who had to tell me I couldn't have more money. It must have been terrible to tell twenty-four-year-old me that I could only have a thousand more dollars on top of my $40K. I made a point to never, ever bring up someone's age in a conversation about their salary, but sometimes it was hard not to. No matter how great you are, there is no amount of talent that can be a stand-in for years of experience, and that's something you can't understand until you're on the other side of it.

I've been told from insiders that in the not-so-distant heyday of women's magazines, EICs were paid not just double but probably triple what I made. I can't really imagine getting that kind of money to do a job that is ultimately so fun. I hope they knew how lucky they were.

I've also learned that culturally there's no "right" way to be an ambitious woman. We don't have a lot of models for young female leadership, and many people's first instinct is to be suspicious of that kind of drive. I've never heard about any of my male coworkers being called entitled when asking for more money. I think if anything it probably gains them respect.

I eventually mastered little tricks to make myself appear older: wide-legged pants and heels, glasses, a cool-toned platinum bob, face makeup, square red nails, consciously removing "um" from my vocabulary, etc. Gradually, though, that aesthetic became less a role I was playing and more of a reflection of who I truly was. There was no longer a need to try to trick people into thinking I was qualified for my job—I knew that I was.

Once my twenties were over, I got asked, "Aren't you a little young?" less and less. Instead, my staff, especially the ones just out of college, teased me for not knowing who certain celebrities were or for not knowing how to use the latest Instagram feature. It was interesting to have gone from "too young to be taken seriously" to "too old to be cool" so quickly. Just like there's no right way to have ambition when you're a woman, there's no right age to be; you're either too young or too old with nothing in between. And I was quietly a little bit thrilled to finally be considered too old for certain things; it was a nice excuse to go to bed early and not follow pop culture so closely. Toward the end of my time at *Nylon*, when I'd take the occasional phone call from a recruiter, and they'd ask me how much money I'd need to be offered to leave my job, I'd tell them the highest number I could say without laughing, and they took me seriously. And being taken seriously was priceless.

4

Low-Rise

I started high school in 2003. George W. Bush was president, and it was the year the war in Iraq began; meanwhile, late-term abortion was banned, and gay marriage remained illegal. The government was pushing for abstinence-only education in public schools. *Nylon* had existed for four years, and Lil' Kim was the only black woman with a cover. *The Simple Life* starring Paris Hilton and Nicole Richie premiered. White indie crossed over into the mainstream, with hits like "Such Great Heights" by the Postal Service, "Maps" by the Yeah Yeah Yeahs, and "12:51" by The Strokes. Late-night infomercials promoted Girls Gone Wild. The earnestness and PC culture of the '90s was replaced with hipster irony.

It was also around the time that low-rise jeans became not just trendy but ubiquitous. My favorite pair was from Delia's:

stretchy, faded blue/gray denim, with zipper pockets and slightly flared ankles that dragged on the floor so much that the hem was frayed and mud stained. They buttoned just above my pubic line and—as was the style at the time—my colorful Victoria's Secret thong was pretty much always whale-tailing out the back.

As a Jewish teenager on Long Island in the early aughts, you had two major style camps to fall into. You could be Jappy (Jewish American Princessy) and indicate that with rolled-down yoga pants (Solo or Hard Tail) or Juicy Couture velour sets and engraved Tiffany jewelry—the precursor to a style that today would be called "basic"—or you could be emo, illustrated with a band T-shirt layered over a long-sleeve shirt, under a black hoodie, with Converse or Saucony sneakers. I was a fifty-fifty hybrid, with a black studded belt barely holding my skinny jeans above my butt crack, bat mitzvah jewelry layered over a Saves The Day shirt, or a Free People dress with combat boots. I wore Hot by Ralph Lauren, a fragrance that came in a vibrant purple bottle and smelled like vanilla and fig on a sweaty summer day. I used Benefit's BADgal black eyeliner to fill in my lower waterline (no mascara). My hair was parted down the middle and hung to my waist; I used a CHI flat iron to kill any life it might have had. The next year I'd cut it all off into a spiky pixie and then streak it with purple.

My freshman year I signed myself up for the yearbook club's photo team. One guy on staff who was a senior took it upon himself to teach me how to use a digital camera and edit in Photoshop. I turned out to be pretty good at it, and so it was assumed that I might take the helm someday. I remember he wore a lot of expensive-looking sweatpants and a thin gold chain, and he smelled like Abercrombie & Fitch. He had a superhot, superskinny girlfriend who was always mad at him.

One day after school we were all in the yearbook room, and I was crouching down in front of the cabinets trying to find a book when I felt something cold and hard press into my skin. I jumped up and found him on the floor behind me, laughing hysterically. He had put a penny in my butt crack, which I guess had been showing while I was crouching, thanks to my low-rise jeans. Behind him was a group of guys, also laughing.

I don't remember what exactly I said, but I do remember feeling my entire body turn splotchy and red, and I know that he told me to calm down, to lighten up, to take a joke. A few weeks later, when his girlfriend finally dumped him, he pulled me into an empty classroom and offered me a back massage that ended with his hands up my shirt. I didn't say no, but I definitely hadn't said yes, either, and was instead frozen with embarrassment. I was fourteen.

He started texting me late at night, texts that I'd read under my blankets on my flip phone. I worried that if I didn't go along with it, he would stop teaching me Photoshop, so I led him on for a while, realizing also that I had a little bit of control; he seemed to actually, in a weird way, like me. But after a few awkward weeks of me fumbling through flirtation, I think he understood that I wasn't ever going to hook up with him, and we stopped speaking. I taught myself more Photoshop, and the next year I became the official photo editor of the yearbook anyway.

I'd had a middle school "boyfriend" before that situation who'd tried for the better part of a year to have oral sex with me, unsuccessfully. I never would have considered myself a prude, but my sexual experiences were truly limited to the ones in my head, which in turn never went past daydreams about kissing. I didn't know what to make of the way boys were treating my body. They seemed to feel entitled to it, like the mere fact of my presence meant they were owed something, and I understood that this simultaneously gave me power and rendered me powerless.

To this day I can't think about low-rise pants without feeling the ghost of a penny being forced into my butt crack, and the subsequent laugher; as Dr. Christine Blasey Ford put it to the Senate in 2018, "Indelible to the hippocampus is the laughter. The uproarious laughter . . ."

I was coming of age in a time when everything was hypersexualized, but I didn't understand the relationship between that and actual sex, a disconnect that's one of the main reasons I didn't realize I was gay until after high school: it was like being disembodied. There was no connection between the performance sexiness and my own pleasure, because I legitimately didn't feel any, even by myself. I might have worn low-rise jeans to look "hot," but I wasn't thinking about wearing them to look *sexy*, though I suppose that was the effect they had, buttoning dangerously close to the top of my (also low-rise) underwear. (In her book *Female Chauvinist Pigs*, about American culture in the early 2000s, journalist Ariel Levy described a similar phenomenon among the female teenagers she interviewed— a disconnect between the performance of sexiness and feelings of pleasure—which she attributed to the contradiction between the push for abstinence-only education and the inescapable raunchiness of pop culture. While she was researching and observing, I was living it.)

Low-rise jeans looked good on me at first, but only because I had started puberty just two years before, and I had yet to develop hips, or cellulite, or a stomach, really. The female celebrities who wore them also had adolescent bodies—long, flat tummies and tiny butts, without any back fat or love handles. Over the next couple of years as hormones raged through me, I got that teenager puffiness, which included a belly, and suddenly those low-rise pants became my enemy. Not wearing them didn't occur to me. Instead I took to wearing them with bulky knit sweaters or zipped-up hoodies, anything to hide the soft flesh that piled up above that tight waistband. I was often accidentally ripping off the belt loops trying to pull my jeans up over my love handles. Eventually I realized they'd fit right if I simply didn't eat until dinner for enough days and then weeks in a row, so that's what I did.

The idea of body positivity had not entered the mainstream. I understood that it was "bad" to have an eating disorder, and I think I noticed Dove's Campaign for Real Beauty, but it was also the time of Destiny's Child, Britney Spears, Kate Hudson, Keira Knightley, and Paris Hilton, and all their teeny-tiny bodies with their long, flat stomachs, hollow between their pointy hip bones. Fat women were mocked mercilessly in movies, on TV, and in real life. Fat jokes were just jokes. I was "lucky" to be a skinny-ish teenager, even though I had to go hungry to get there; the trendiest jeans actually came in my size.

In hindsight I'm struck by the relationship between the clothes that were in style, the hypersexualized, nearly pornographic celebrity culture, and the political climate. I was too young to be aware of how closely everything was related, and further, how subject to change they'd be; as a young teenager my reality felt like the only one that had ever existed. There was just one world, one set of values, one acceptable way to have a body, one cool way to dress it.

I was finally able to vote in the 2008 election, which meant I got to cast my first-ever ballot for Barack Obama during my sophomore year of college. We were in the middle of what journalists told us was the worst economic crisis since the Great Depression, and Obama's campaign message was simple: HOPE. We sorely needed it. For the first time in my life I felt a connection to a politician; here was a relatively young person who talked about things like women's equality and had crowds chanting "Yes we can!" Like my generation, he was on social media. He was against gay marriage at that point but also said he would be open to discussing it, which was definitely more than what Bush had said. (Bush had, in fact, proposed an amendment to the Constitution that would ban it forever, while it was already illegal.) I had started dating girls just a few months before the election and was suddenly painfully aware of how my life would be impacted by the personal beliefs of lawmakers.

My coming out was also timed to the boyfriend jeans trend—blissfully soft and saggy straight-legged pants with generous pockets that looked fine no matter what I'd eaten or how close I was to my period. As a new lesbian, and someone who came out in the context of a relationship, not a community, I had no idea how to go about finding my people. I wanted nothing more than to be visible to others, and the tomboy silhouette of a boyfriend jean helped a lot. Plus, they were so comfortable, and physical comfort acted as a metaphor for how it felt to realize I was gay. There was power in jeans that fit. It was a new kind of sexiness, one that was outside of any sort of male gaze.

I wasn't sure what exactly my gender presentation should be, though. I'd always been so feminine, and when I came out, I was generally attracted to other feminine girls, but they seemed to only be interested in me when I was dressed androgynously. I took to wearing my boyfriend jeans with gray or black Hanes tank tops, the kind you buy in bulk from Kmart, and stopped wearing a bra. I started shaving parts of my head and then eventually all of it. Being visibly queer made me feel more my-self than I ever had, even if I had yet to fully nail down where my femininity fit within it.

Although I felt physically comfortable in soft, saggy jeans and tank tops, I soon realized I wasn't sending the right mes-sage. I remember once bringing a woman home with me from a party, and when she entered my bedroom, she looked around at the mess of makeup and products and exclaimed, "Oh my god. You're such a *girl!*" I decided in that moment that I hated her. And also that I needed to dress more femininely if I wanted to be seen for who I fully was.

Around that time, at a queer poetry event put on by NYU, I spotted a woman who looked like no one I'd ever seen be-fore. She was the tallest person in the cluster of girls she was talking to and had long, bleached-blonde hair. She was wearing red lipstick and high-waisted jeans with a thin cotton tank top tucked in. When she lifted her arms, soft patches of blonde arm-pit hair were revealed. She caught me staring at her and smiled. That night she sent me a friend request on Facebook and asked me out. We went on a few dates before she completely ghosted me. It was for the best, though: It wasn't so much that I was attracted to her. It was that I finally had an example of how I wanted to look. I had never really seen someone who was so feminine and so clearly gay.

She was also, as it turned out, a trendsetter. No one was wearing high-waisted pants yet. But within a few years, with

Obama in the White House for a second term and equal rights for women and minorities on the horizon, high-waisted pants settled over everything like a warm blanket. A shape that flatters hips and booties, high-waisted jeans seemed to be designed with actual curves in mind—the way they encompassed that part of your lower back that isn't technically your butt but isn't not your butt, either, and how the front held your whole belly, holding it in or expanding with it but either way not cutting it off.

This, too, was good timing for my personal life: I was ready to return to the femininity that felt the most natural to me, and I had realized that the women I liked most didn't really care at all about the rise of my jeans.

As my understanding of my own gender evolved, so too did the high-waisted pants trend, which changed over a few years from skinny ankles to wide-leg trousers. Suddenly, the bigger your pants were, the better. It was the opposite of what I'd grown up with: whereas I remember going to Delia's and squeezing myself into the tiniest, skinniest lowest rises I could find, I was now looking for exaggerated widths. It was a game-changer, one that happened in tandem with a developing awareness about the ways in which the fashion industry had led women to think our bodies were fundamentally flawed by not designing clothes for curvy bodies. My first story for *Nylon* print in 2014 was about wearing wide-fit clothing and how powerful it could be to intentionally take up space.

But high-waisted pants weren't without complications. They weren't always comfortable; we went from bisecting our stomachs with a low-rise waistband to hoisting them up and zipping them away entirely. In that way they were more traditionally flattering but harder to eat in, and harder still to sit in for a long workday. Jesse Kamm, the designer credited with truly bringing the high-waisted silhouette to the masses with her 2013 debut of the now cult-classic sailor pants, later made headlines again when women began pointing out that her pants don't run above a size 12, limiting the women who can benefit from the high-waisted, wide-leg shape to the same ones that could enjoy low-rise pants. For plus-size women, the progression from low-rise to high-rise didn't seem like progress at all.

Similarly, the sociopolitical progress made under Obama turned out to not be as widely celebrated as those of us living in progressive bubbles liked to believe—bubbles that were popped in 2016, when we were all so sure we were about to witness the election of the first-ever female president. I wanted Hillary Clinton to win so badly that it felt like an ache. I read the overtly sexist reporting on the election with a pit in my stomach. During the debates when Trump would loom over her menacingly, I wanted to scream, *Run!* But I also didn't want her to run away; I needed her to stay and fight. Trump was the embodiment of every guy who had ever assaulted me or bullied me or harassed me, and he was being taken seriously.

I was in Lisbon, Portugal, by myself, when he won the

election. I had cast my absentee ballot and then left the country for a tech conference called Web Summit with fifty thousand attendees. I was moderating two panels, one with the founders of famous music festivals and another with a DJ. I'd agreed to the latter because I'd been told that the DJ was trans and an active part of the community in Portugal, which sounded really interesting—it was only once I got there that I realized it was a miscommunication thanks to the language barrier: he was a *trance* DJ. And an active member of the Portuguese trance community.

At any rate, I went to bed at midnight on Election Day, which was about six p.m. at home, expecting to wake up to a new feminist world. All my friends were having election-viewing parties. I woke up at seven a.m. to hundreds of texts, and under the covers with one eye open, I frantically tried to figure out what had happened. I scrolled through my Instagram timeline (which was still chronological) and watched as everyone's joyful selfies from their parties devolved into drunken sorrow. When I finally put the pieces together, I sobbed. Eventually I pulled some clothes on and made my way deliriously to the hotel's breakfast buffet, where all around me I could hear people murmuring in different languages, the word "Trump" the only one I understood. I'd never felt so alone in my life.

On my way home, when the plane landed, people in "Make America Great Again" hats chanted, "USA! USA!" And then, at the immigration window at JFK Airport, I got stopped by border security. Thanks to the way I'd changed my look so many times over the past decade, my hair in my passport photo was long and dark brown, and in person it was short and blonde. They didn't think my passport was mine. They asked for additional ID, but in my driver's license photo, my head was shaved. They asked me in patronizing tones how often I went to the hair salon. I was jet-lagged and hungry and not in the mood to be taunted by uniformed men, and I couldn't rein in my attitude. They ended up detaining me for several hours in a small windowless room. Finally I was brought into an office where a man at a computer asked me detailed questions to verify my identity. He eventually asked me for my paternal grandfather's address and decided to let me go when I said, "He's dead."

I texted about it with a friend on the way back to Brooklyn, and she said, "Babe, welcome to Trump's America."

Trump's election to office wasn't just a win for Republicans; it was a win for men everywhere who thought they should be able to grab women "by the pussy." His power made way for everyone's down-low sexism, racism, and homophobia to be aired. In 2017, the FBI reported the highest surge in hate crimes since 9/11. There were nazi rallies across the country. Even in New York City, it felt suddenly unsafe to exist, especially on the subways, where I was attacked physically and verbally by men multiple times. Once while I was on the way to work holding hands with my girlfriend, Wallace, a man spit on us.

The social media activism that flourished under Obama

took hold in a new way, with women using Twitter and Instagram to organize global marches. Perhaps because it felt like there was nothing we could do about Trump, women had other targets, taking down serial rapist Harvey Weinstein, and then the #MeToo movement gained traction, which had women calling out abusers across industries. Social media became a place to perform political views that were no longer represented in government. In response, women in media, especially women of color, self-identified feminists, Jews, and queers, saw an increase in death threats online, but it did little to quell the movement; if anything, the death threats validated its importance.

Part of the political performance on social media for progressives included the integration of body positivity into social justice content. Inspired by the work of fat activists, women began tagging their curvy selfies with #effyourbeautystandards and #selflove. The problem, though, was that thin women were doing it, too; women whose bodies were probably never marginalized for their size wanted in on the self-love, seeking validation for their insecurities through means created by women who were actually oppressed for the way they looked. Body parts got hashtagged. Even though the skinny-driven #thighgap was replaced in popularity with #thighbrow, the name for a line that sometimes appears on women at the top of their thighs when they kneel, through this labeling of body types, a hierarchy was implied. For every person who saw themselves reflected in a trending body part hashtag, someone did not.

Even before hashtags, women's body parts have been going in and out of style for as long as there's been style. What's meant by that, really, is that for the moment, people with a certain physical characteristic are privileged. When I was a teenager, it was stomachs. Everyone wanted a six-pack. The best way to show your flat stomach off was with low-rise jeans; they were especially cool looking if you were skinny enough to have your jeans reveal the top of a V-shaped muscle that started at your hip points and ended just out of sight.

Later, when the Kardashian sisters rose to fame, big butts became cool—a shape that tends to look fabulous in a high-rise waist. But the thing is that our body types don't change with the trends; big boobs, for example, are sometimes in and sometimes out, which changes what you'll see on the runways and in ads, but people with flat chests like me—unless they have surgery—remain the same and therefore are allegedly sometimes cool and sometimes not. It's a sneaky way to make sure someone is always feeling like garbage, while other people are celebrated for simply being born into a certain body that happens to fit well into the newest clothing.

Lest any one kind of woman get used to her body type being in style, now that Kim Kardashian fandom has shifted to Kendall and Kylie, her younger, less curvy half sisters, and their circle of supermodel / pop star BFFs, fashion has begun creeping back to the shapes I grew up with, like low-rise jeans paired with crop tops to show a long expanse of flat stomach between the two. This time, though, you have to have the skinny stomach *with* wide-set hips and a bootie, an exaggerated hourglass shape that looks best when squatting or kneeling. It's most noticeable within what I've heard called the "Instagram Generation."

Instagram as a whole has been a site of reincarnation for the campy trashiness of celebrities in the early aughts through younger and younger up-and-comers—models and DJs and pop singers—who engage in nostalgia for an era that they are probably too young to fully remember. Fashion is generally understood to have a twenty-year cycle, so just as the 2010s was all things '90s, the second Roaring '20s will show a resurrection of Bush-era aesthetics, and maybe sooner than anticipated: fashion writers started to predict the return of low-rise pants as early as 2017. There had been a few moments on various runways that foreshadowed it, and interviews with executives at major denim brands revealed they were reinvesting in the silhouette. It seemed astounding that a style that had been largely accepted as uncomfortable and impractical could simply be brought back, just like that. But notably, we also once again had a president who didn't respect women, in a "one step forward, five steps back" dance that makes progress feel incredibly delayed. In so many ways we circled back to before we liberated our love handles with higher rises.

When news of the low-rise return began trending online, the internet at large seemed to react with one giant "NOOOO" in unison. No one wants this, we screamed at our screens, as though we were powerless to stop the return of this trend that looks good on approximately 0.00001 percent of the population (statistics my own).

But here's the thing. We weren't powerless. Before digital media infiltrated the fashion industry, and specifically the trends to come out of Fashion Week, editors and designers could make decisions in a vacuum. What was cool or not cool had an air of mystery to it; what's more, it was presented as a truth. A trend was agreed upon and then it was in stores and then everyone wanted it. But we know better now. No matter what your day job is, you can watch Fashion Week unfold pretty much in real time on your iPhone. There's almost complete transparency into the moments that dictate trends. So this time around, armed with insight and not-too-distant memories, the generation that's been shamed so much for our reliance on our technology—my generation—has more power than ever before. The same way social media has given us insight into politics and helped fuel the #resistance, we can use it to fight back. But will we?

In many ways Instagram is an equal-opportunity social media platform, in that it positions celebrities and regular people alongside each other in the same feed. With the exception of the little blue checkmark to indicate a verified account, meaning you are who you say you are, it's a pretty effective equalizer. We all get the same amount of space and the same tools, and we show up in the same feed, leading us to feel as though the celebrities we see are our friends, or at least like the images we see of them are authentic. Its popularity also feels like a response to frustration over seeing heavily doctored images of women in pop culture; it's a place where we can post images of ourselves on our own terms. I think part of what was so appealing about following celebrities on Instagram was, at first, that it allowed them to get ahead of the paparazzi-driven hunger to catch them off guard and photograph them off duty by posting themselves off duty first. And for a while it was delightful to see professionally beautiful people in no makeup and sweatpants with their loved ones.

The platform gives everyone—celebrity or otherwise—total control over the images of themselves that are published for the world to see, but in reality, once we have that control, we haven't found ourselves implementing the lessons we've learned about the way Photoshop and runway models have affected Western female self-esteem; instead, we use filters, and then as other apps were developed, we got Facetune, a kind of Photoshop-for-dummies application that lets you change pretty much whatever you want on your own face and body. Once people realized that just because you're posting it yourself doesn't mean you can't change it, Instagram was never going to be the authentic, intimate platform it pretends to be. I am absolutely positive that the majority of the images that celebrities and influencers post of themselves are doctored in some way, especially the very young, very popular ones, who are models and usually daughters of other celebrities, with impossibly thin waists, out-of-proportion booties, and skin as clear as glass.

So, as the platform grew and photos became easy to manipulate, the vibe switched from "See? Nobody is perfect!" to, "Actually, look how perfect I am."

Depending on who you follow, you could easily curate your feed to confirm a universal sneaking suspicion: that everybody is perfect but you. The result is the result that's always been. We know the end of this story, although the characters have changed. When you're barraged with images of women who have hyperidealized bodies, you start to forget that it's not the same as being healthy, and you start to aspire to look like that. Instagram for me has become as toxic as, if not more so than, the runway—runway casting at least doesn't pretend to represent real life.

But it's not just that people are pretending to reflect their real lives on Instagram—it's that they're showing their *best* lives, curating a highlight reel. There's pressure to do it, too, as though the value of your success, whether professional or personal, can be measured in how well your iPhone captures it. It's competitive, exhausting, addicting, all encompassing. It hinges on virtue signaling. It sets us all up to fail.

And ultimately as a result it's become harder and harder to tell the difference between what's real and what's enhanced. I'm constantly alarmed when I meet influencers in real life because of how different they look, even though they post close-up images of their faces. But truthfully, it's hard *not* to change your own self, even just a little bit—I do use Facetune, albeit lightly, but still; it's difficult for me to post a photo of myself with a shiny forehead or a zit if I could just blur it out. A friend recently said to me that she loves the app because she can reshape part of her nose that she's always hated. For her, it's an alternative to plastic surgery, because her nose only bothers her when she sees it in photos, so why have to see it at all?

But, okay: not everyone does this. The true body-positive community on Instagram—the one that puts fat acceptance front and center—continues to champion women's bodies in a way that is definitely pushing us in the right direction. And I'm sure a lot of my analysis of the phenomenon comes from my own competitiveness and my own struggle to redefine perfection for myself. Or maybe my struggle is to step outside of the confines of perfection altogether and generate self-esteem that isn't rooted in comparison. That's something I am very much still working on.

I don't hashtag my body parts, because I understand objectively that I am thin and therefore probably no one cares how I feel about my body, and rightfully so; it wouldn't be empowering to the women who follow me to read me ramble about how much I #love my body. It would just be annoying. The fact that I've been to hell and back to feel something adjacent to comfortable with myself is mostly irrelevant; thin privilege is attached to your exterior, not your interior, no matter how difficult that interior is to live within.

As women's media grapples with how to be more positive

and inclusive while covering topics like fashion and beauty, I frequently find myself caught between two worlds—the world of empowerment culture and the world of perfectionism. At the intersection of these two things is the idea that everybody is already perfect and that there is power in owning your self-worth as is, which is, I think, the ideal at the heart of contemporary pop culture feminism. The further away from empowerment the idea of perfection gets, the more you enter spaces where women still talk about their weight-loss goals and fat-shame other people. The further away from perfection culture you get, the closer you are to a value system that takes women's aesthetics out of the equation entirely. Neither extreme works for me.

The common denominator, though, is that both ways of viewing the world are grounded in a digital performance of feminism. I'm suspicious of any political view where the focus is on the public branding and not the real-life experience. But the flip side is that in curating our feminist brands, regardless of how you define that, we are allowed to create our own narratives, with ourselves at the center—rather than ourselves as inevitable by-products of a world we can't control. We're no longer passive consumers of culture; we don't have to engage with trends if they don't serve us. Nor should we. Especially not those of us who remember going hungry to squeeze into a denim shape designed for emaciated figures.

I don't love the "women have more important things to worry about" argument against fashion; I believe there is value in what we wear and how it makes us feel. Generations before us, women fought for the right to wear pants. Now we need to make sure those pants don't make us want to starve, don't punish us for eating a nice big lunch, and can be worn by all of us. The argument, really, is that we need clothes more befitting of women who are trying their damnedest to live their best lives while changing the world in the process—regardless of how they choose to hashtag it, if at all. And if low-rise jeans really do become cool again, I'll have no problem sitting it out. After all, if trends are cyclical, it won't last forever. Maybe it's my thirties talking, but I'd rather be off trend than uncomfortable. And anyway, who I am has nothing to do with how my jeans fit.

5

Everybody Else Is Perfect

It was June 2017, a precious time of year in New York City when the heat has yet to vaporize the garbage juice, so the air still smells like pollen and possibility. Hyperphotogenic pink-gold clouds appeared every evening just in time for me to emerge at the top of the subway stairs after work, sweaty and exhausted, phone in my hand.

In Bed-Stuy, Brooklyn, where I lived, the ice-cream truck song was always blaring in the background, no matter what time of day it was, harmonizing hauntingly with the urgent giggles and shouts of children—which sounded charming but, if you listened closely, were full of insults and curses, hurled joyfully at one another. It was perfect weather for a soft, loose T-shirt tucked into even softer jeans, for men to linger outside of bodegas watching you walk by, and for the collective seasonal depression to be instantly replaced with boundless passion for a city that everyone probably just swore they hated.

I was on a third date with Wallace, a friend who had recently admitted to sharing the crush I'd had on her since we met a few years earlier. We'd been to this candlelit, overpriced neighborhood bar countless times separately, and a couple of times together as part of a group. The most recent time had been on our first date, when we were both so nervous we stared past each other at the rows of liquor bottles, the occasional nanosecond of eye contact so overwhelming that we both tried to avoid it. But by date three, maybe because we'd been casual friends for so many years before, we'd quickly fallen into tell-each-other-everything territory, and I was going full speed ahead, divulging all the gory details of a breakup with a woman I'd been with for a year. The split had culminated in a daylong feelings marathon during which she insisted, repeatedly, that I was not in the right frame of mind to decide to end our relationship because—as she so bluntly put it—"You have a mental illness." It was cruel but not necessarily untrue, which a friend later joked meant she'd gone "full Scorpio" on me.

Maybe it's because I'd had two negronis, but I then found myself admitting a detail to Wallace that I had only recently begun to say out loud: "It got complicated because I had taken a little break from food." I said it casually, like I was kind of joking, not wanting to sound dramatic.

Everyone else so far had regarded this admission with alarm, which was annoying, or skepticism, which was more annoying. Wallace, though, matched my tone. "Oh yeah?" she said. "That's no good. You kind of need food."

"Yeah," I laughed, relieved. "As it turns out, you really do need to eat things."

Her knee was touching mine under the bar, sending an electrical current through my leg and up my spine. We ordered six oysters and two double cheeseburgers with fries. It was the biggest meal I'd had in months, but I didn't tell her that.

No one really knew: When you work in fashion (and, probably, anywhere), weight loss is rewarded with compliments and attention. No matter how thin I got, my friends, coworkers, and even acquaintances "couldn't believe" how "good" I looked. Meanwhile, I had a doctor, a nutritionist, and a therapist working together to help me start eating regularly. I was about three months into recovery from what I was told was anorexia.

It's estimated that upwards of thirty million people in the United States have an eating disorder. Meanwhile, it's also estimated that more than 70 percent of them won't seek treatment because of stigma. This statistic feels especially prescient: In this golden age of female empowerment, we aren't supposed to have eating disorders anymore. It's not cool to hate your body. Women, and especially women within the public eye, are

obligated to promote a message of self-love, to put all our cellulite and wrinkles and rolls out there proudly. Culturally, we're all
about "wellness" and redefining it on our own terms. And yet,
studies show that eating disorder rates continue to rise.

I've moved in and out of periods of disordered eating for as
long as I can remember, though I can never tell it's happening
until I'm on the other side. When you admit to having an eating
disorder, you're also admitting that you're body negative in an
aggressively body-positive world. You've prioritized impossible
beauty standards over your own health. And ultimately—despite
your feminist politics—you've internalized the patriarchy. The
misogyny that says women need to be skinny has infiltrated
your brain until you believe it, until it feels like it's a belief system you organically hold. It's oppression at its most sinister: so
pervasive that it becomes part of you. By starving yourself, or
making yourself throw up, or otherwise doing whatever you
can to keep your body small, you are in effect working to uphold the values of a system built on keeping you down.

That is, at least, what I told myself, what I punished myself
with, and what many others do, too; I think it's probably why
many people don't want to talk about their eating disorders in
today's world, which can feel built on surface-level feminism
depending on what bubble you live in. For me, saying it out
loud was nothing short of devastating, especially because a
huge part of my mission as an editor had been to help young
women expunge patriarchy both from their own minds and

their communities. I had built a career around pushing the boundaries of beauty standards. I would fight to the death for every woman's right to representation in media—regardless of her size, race, sexual identity, where she comes from. And I knew firsthand what it felt like to not see yourself represented and how lonely it could be—like it is for many people, my first memory of magazines is of flipping through them and not seeing anyone I identified with. I could talk forever about the importance of diversity in fashion. But at a certain point, it became myself that I was fighting against, too: for whatever reason, no matter how strongly I advocated for other women, I left myself out of it.

It felt like admitting weakness: I was trying so hard to be the picture-perfect empowered millennial woman, but I had gotten stuck on the "picture perfect" part. In my darkest days, I tried to find balance: every time I did something particularly crazy, like only drinking liquids for a day's nutrition, I yelled at my social media team about not having enough body diversity on Instagram.

In a fabulous essay for Racked titled "Body Positivity Is a Scam," Amanda Mull writes that the original definition of the phrase, as a tenet of the fat acceptance movement, is this: "To have a body that's widely reviled and discriminated against and love it anyway, in the face of constant cultural messaging about your flaws, is subversive." Her argument is that this concept has been co-opted by corporations that have discovered women are more likely to share their content, thus creating free advertising, if it's based on empowerment, not shame. And when it's used as a marketing tactic by these corporations, especially within social media, Mull writes, "an alarming percentage of the public conversation about which bodies our culture values or rejects pivots around models, actresses, and other professionally beautiful people reassuring what they seem to believe is a dubious public that they are, in fact, super hot."

In the end, the loudest, most body-positive voices end up belonging to those whose bodies aren't actually all that marginalized—mainly, thin white women, whose voices drown out the women of color who were doing the work long before them. It's a confusing fusion of empowerment culture and white privilege, and it becomes a much less powerful conversation than originally intended. The ultimate message is that women have to be all things at once—publicly supportive of all bodies, yet representative of the impossible ideal.

In our newly woke world of marketing based on "positivity," the blame is once again placed on women—but this time, it's not our bodies that are wrong; it's our *feelings about our bodies*.

And my feelings about my body were definitely wrong, creating a vortex of shame. By the time I finally started to realize I had a problem, I was twenty-seven and thinner than I'd ever been. I hadn't weighed myself but knew from the way my clothes were fitting (or rather, not fitting) that something was wrong. I'd later find out that I was around one hundred pounds (twenty-five to thirty less than my regular weight). I had gained and lost a ton of weight in rapid succession over a two-year period, as I reorganized my personal life through breakups and moving and job changes. It wasn't super intentional—I don't remember actively trying to be skinny so much as focusing on my diet and exercise as things I could control when the rest of my life felt so uncertain and scary. What started as a coping strategy turned obsessive, and I completely lost touch with my own ability to feel hunger.

It was having a real impact on my day-to-day. I felt tired all the time. I cried often for no apparent reason, especially on the subway or after working out. Dark circles settled under my eyes, and my hair got so thin that I got extensions glued in to fake the appearance of thickness. I lied a lot, usually about having plans when really I was going to work out. The one thrill became shopping, because suddenly clothes designed for models hung on my body the way they were designed to; things like loose sack dresses and high-high-waisted trousers maintained their own shape. Once I realized that if I skipped a meal the hunger would go away after a few hours, I didn't see why I'd ever need to really eat again.

It was easy to disappear into the demanding hours of my job, and then it was easy to disappear from my own life entirely. I was like a ghost. And for a while I got away with it. My friends and family believed me when I said I was too busy with work to do anything else.

Eventually, though, multiple people started to notice my size and comment on it. It started with a concerned text from my mom: "Why do you look so skinny on Instagram?"

I was at work. I remember typing slowly: "I feel like maybe I've caught an eating disorder, like a cold," I sent. Later that night I told the Scorpio, my then-girlfriend, about the exchange, and to my surprise she grew angry, frustrated with my reticence. "You *definitely* have an eating disorder," she snapped, and then listed off my symptoms—my lack of energy, bad moods, workout addiction. Then she landed the ultimate blow: "Why do you *need* to be so skinny?"

I had no answer, just embarrassed silence. It felt like asking me for the answer to the root of anorexia. I slowly started to tell my inner circle what was going on, and this angry, frustrated, questioning reaction kept repeating. People, it seems, get really annoyed about eating disorders: *But you're so skinny.* They're even more annoyed by the process of recovery. Once you've labeled the problem, people want you to be able to just fix it.

I had a couple of very supportive friends who had struggled with their own relationship to food, including my friend Lindsey, a woman I'd met through work who lived in LA. As a photographer—someone who professionally focuses on aesthetics—she and I had what felt like an instant understanding of each other. In addition to an incredibly rewarding creative relationship (she became my go-to photographer for *Nylon* cover shoots), she was one of my only friends who consistently saw through whatever veneer I tried to hide behind, and would call me on it gently.

For the most part, though, I was too embarrassed to tell my peers about it. And except for a few extremely worried phone calls from my parents, my family gradually stopped talking to me about it, too, especially once I reassured them that I was getting the help I needed. The sick part of my brain wondered if I was just never skinny enough for it to truly be a concern.

In hindsight I realize that they felt I had intentionally pushed them away—I'd react with what looked like annoyance when they'd check in on me. I was far from annoyed, though; I was feeling a combination of guilt over burdening them with worry and resentment for said worry. But they were trying to respect the boundaries they thought I was setting. I didn't know how to ask for help, and because I was so independent and professionally successful, very few people realized I needed it.

In reality I felt totally alone, and I felt like it was all my fault. I had failed in keeping up with the self-love that my generation was supposed to be so famous for. What's more, I totally understood the frustration and annoyance that was directed my way—I'd felt it toward other people. I had a friend in college who was about six inches shorter than me and *at least* thirty pounds lighter. One day while we were getting ready to go to class, she stood in front of her mirror and said something to the effect of, "I'm so ashamed of how fat I've gotten."

I was irritated. She was the furthest thing from fat I'd ever seen. So I said, "If you think you're fat, what do you think of me?"

She was stunned. "I think you're perfect," she said.

"I'm twice your size," I exclaimed. "I literally loom over you."

She started to cry. "I know I have a problem," she said. "I think everyone else is so perfect and beautiful, and I just think I'm so ugly."

At the time I thought I didn't understand. But then, I was thinking the same exact thing: I felt enormous and disgusting, too. Yet I had started to date girls and many of them were curvier than me; if anything, I found myself attracted to their softness. I remember one girl I was dating complaining to me about a little weight gain around her thighs and my honest response was, "But that just means there's more of you, and that's such a good thing!" My own body, though, was a different story— I was keeping myself on a tight leash, convinced that if I gained weight no one would want me. I was completely unaware that this was problematic thinking, because it just felt so true. In hindsight, it was true for my friend as well.

This is all pretty textbook body dysmorphia. Women with eating disorders don't see themselves accurately, so whereas they can think other women are beautiful at any size, that thinking doesn't extend to their own reflection. People who *don't* have eating disorders seem to have a hard time empathizing with that. It's hard to wrap your brain around someone having certain requirements for themselves but not for other people.

I've always thought the women I love, whether it's friends, family, or girlfriends, are the most beautiful people in the world. When they criticize their own appearances, it hurts my feelings—if only they could see what I see. It also calls into question this issue of perspective, which I keep coming back to: *If you think that about yourself, what do you think of me?* To which the answer, again and again, is that different standards apply. I'm trying to avoid cliché here, but I really do think we could all benefit from seeing ourselves the way the people who love us do.

Which brings me back to the aforementioned Scorpio. Mid-breakup, she made me promise to tell my therapist that I wasn't really eating. I agreed to it; I'd been in therapy for years without bringing up my on-again, off-again eating habits. I didn't want to tell my therapist about it, because I didn't want to stop—I liked having that kind of control over my body. I also didn't really think it was that big of a deal. When I finally told her, she was alarmed, and convinced me to see a doctor so we could determine how severe it was based on test results. She sent me to a physician who specialized in eating disorders in adolescent girls.

The day before I went, I wondered if I should eat more so that she wouldn't think I had a problem, or if I should eat less so that she would take me seriously. I went alone, not wanting to burden anyone with what felt like a self-imposed disaster. I was definitely the oldest person in the waiting room, besides the moms accompanying their teenage daughters. When I filled out the intake forms, there was an entire page for my parents' information. I asked the receptionist if she really needed my mother's phone number, and she studied my face for a minute before saying I could skip it.

The doctor diagnosed me with anorexia quickly. I was mortified but also relieved; I was exhausted from being hungry all the time, and now there was a professional telling me I needed to eat more, or else. There was also something so soothing about having someone tell me what I had to do—I had been making my whole life up as I went, including how I took care of myself, and she lifted the burden. There were, in fact, rules to follow in order to stay alive; I actually couldn't just go without eating indefinitely.

Years of therapy have clarified for me the connection between my relationship to food and my coping mechanisms, or rather my lack thereof. Being skinny was a weapon, a strategy, a safety net. Trying to lose weight was a convenient way to distract myself from what was really going on.

It was also, and maybe most importantly, a secret so easy to deny because there was so much evidence to the contrary: my work, for one. Being gay came in a close second. Queer people are so inclusive, so all about supporting all kinds of bodies— right? Socially, I was part of a world where fatness had been reclaimed. Queer fat femmes and butches were lavished with as much positive attention as everyone else. They were celebrated. And I celebrated them, too. I just didn't think my own body could be included.

And I knew that once it wasn't a secret, I would be obligated to get it under control, and at first I really didn't want to: Why would I try to gain weight when I'd worked so hard to lose it? As I was told, though, that was the eating disorder talking.

After a round of blood tests on that first visit, the doctor called me and said that I needed to gain ten pounds to be at the minimum weight for my height, in order to not do permanent damage to my body. All my results were low; my estradiol was so minimal that I was barely getting my period, and my vitamins D and B12 were alarming. She also explained that based on how low my T3, or triiodothyronine, levels were, it would take a full two years for my brain to fully recover. T3, she told me, comes from good fats and lines your brain; it makes your synapses connect. Low T3 is a symptom of starvation. It's why it's hard to think when you're hungry. This was the first piece of scare-tactic information that truly got to me. Everything else—the dips in my energy, the potential for disease down the road—I could deal with. I was also struggling with depression, and my existential angst responded *So what?* when presented with mortality.

But I drew the line at a decline in mental capacity. That, to me, was not acceptable. Two years for my brain to bounce back sounded like an eternity. The doctor told me the good news was I'd be able to recover fully as long as I started eating again. Eventually, I did, slowly at first, working with a nutritionist to get back up to three meals a day, then adding snacks, then making sure that every meal was well-rounded and satisfying. They had me incorporate a protein shake into every meal, in little boxed cartons by a brand called Orgain that I ordered online in bulk. The doctor advised that I keep it in a desk drawer because she said it would be recognizable to other people who had eating disorders and that I might want to protect my privacy. A couple of years later, I spotted someone else's Orgain in the work fridge, and my brain raced to figure out who it might belong to.

The doctor didn't take health insurance, and my plan didn't cover my diagnosis in the acceptable out-of-network expenses, so my first visit was $800, my follow-up was $400, and my third visit was another $800; the nutritionist was $150/week, as was my therapist. I couldn't afford both regular doctor visits and the weekly therapist and nutritionist, which was extra motivation to follow the plan they created for me: I hated the thought that my hard-earned salary was all going to treatment. It felt like failure. So I stopped seeing the eating disorder doctor after three visits and stuck with the therapist and nutritionist. I had to relearn how to put meals together, which was humiliating but also incredibly helpful. I surrendered completely to professional care, understanding that my own ideas about health and food were no longer trustworthy.

After outsourcing all my various issues to professionals around Manhattan, I managed to finally feel like I wasn't living from crisis to crisis; I could approach food as something I needed to feel good, not the other way around. And it was from this place that I finally began to admit the hypocrisy that lurked in the shadows of my professional success. It felt almost laughable, if it hadn't gotten so hard, thinking about the standards I held myself to while making content to destroy the very idea of those standards in the first place.

Once I gained the weight and kept it, I started sleeping through the night. Wallace and I had started to talk about moving in together. At work I was filled with so many ideas I could barely contain myself. I was talking over my colleagues in meetings, making lists; I couldn't speak or type fast enough to get all my thoughts out as quickly as they came. I started writing again, and writing, and writing.

I wasn't interested in writing about what it's like to have anorexia, though. I didn't think it was very compelling, and I knew from experience that people struggling with eating disorders tend to twist that kind of writing into how-to guides. I was, however, fascinated by how pervasive it continued to be, even as women's media made leaps and bounds toward being more body positive. It was as though the culture had been fractured with various, intersecting, often conflicting ethoses: From the secret body-image issues of the people creating body-positive content to the frail-framed figures of the latest crop of teenage celebrities, to the powerful activism-focused realm of Generation Zers on Instagram who exposed their bodies to promote a message of self-love—and then their counterparts, the lifestyle bloggers who were either starving in the name of wellness or overusing self-editing apps. On Instagram there were vulnerable confessions from normatively beautiful people who hated their bodies and were claiming hardship, right next to declarations of self-love from plus-size people who were likely actually discriminated against because of their size. Celebrities above a size 4 who went out in public in crop tops were called "brave," as though that was not totally condescending. It became so chaotic. The messages women received, the people creating those messages, and the people featured within the messages were so often at odds with one another and with themselves.

I heard countless women in the industry who didn't fit into the thin/white/straight/cisgender paradigm say that they didn't want anyone else to feel as left out of media as they had. What they were not saying was that they wanted to create a sense of inclusiveness that they themselves could benefit from. It was always for people like them, for the next generation. It got even more complicated when I looked at the return on investment of inclusivity. Brands were benefiting financially from improving the range of women they represented, but they were not really doing the work to acknowledge the problems that they created in the first place.

In 2018, I attended an International Women's Day panel that featured a famous plus-size model who had recently been on a billboard in her underwear. It was a stunning victory for representation, but when asked about it onstage, she said something along the lines of, "It was embarrassing." I was confused. How could someone who was becoming the face of a movement be embarrassed to have her body on display? She was supposed to be bravely leading the charge. Instead she talked about feeling humiliated by her rolls and having to give herself a pep talk before seeing it. And it later came out that the clothing brand, although it used plus-size models in its campaign, did not actually offer sizes that fit them. I began to question everything I'd been told about how to feel about my body, wondering, Is the body-positive movement just another extension of traditional women's work—something we do for other people but not ourselves? And why the fuck don't we?

It's not hard to imagine why women might hate their bodies when our place in the world is so often determined by them, and when so few people actually occupy that highly glorified yet rarely lived place of ultra-thin/straight/white/cisgender privilege. Despite being the majority, plus-size women are discriminated against and often publicly shamed for their appearance, which affects everything from access to effective healthcare to employment to travel to shopping. But thin women, in my experience, balk at admitting to being a privileged category, especially thin white women. I wonder if it's because they're punishing themselves so much to maintain that skinniness that the suffering feels louder than any societal benefit they encounter. But that's a pretty naive way to experience the world, indicative of a privilege so ingrained you hardly realize it's there. It also seems entirely possible that the panic to remain thin stems from a fear of losing that privilege—a maybe subconscious admittance.

It's been over a decade since I watched my gorgeous friend look in the mirror and tell her tiny reflection it was fat. It's troubling to picture editors who chose to glorify images of extremely thin white women in the pages of their magazines; their definition of beauty was so limited and subsequently so harmful to their readers. They made beauty an exclusive class, and we are still dealing with the repercussions, even those of us who try to incorporate body positivity into our understanding of the world. I constantly find myself in conversations with women who—like me—alternate between two extremes: thinking other women are perfect just as they are, and quietly loathing themselves.

Once, at lunch with a colleague, while she was talking to me about her wedding diet, I got distracted by her face: I hadn't really realized that she was as pretty as a Glossier model, with glowy, poreless skin, thick eyebrows, and dark-blonde lashes so elaborate they looked fake. Needing to know her secrets, I interrupted her. "Sorry," I said, "do you have *any* makeup on?"

She blushed. "Just bronzer," and then told me that she can't wear mascara because her eyelashes are too long. Too long! For mascara! I said, "Oh my god. If I looked like you, I would never put a single drop of anything on my face." She looked shocked. She had, after all, been in the middle of telling me about how everyone told her she'd lose weight planning her wedding, but she hadn't yet and so was on a Serious Diet. "But that's what I think about you," she replied.

I rolled my eyes. "I have, like, forty pounds of concealer on," I told her, and quickly brought the subject back to her wedding while we waited for the journalist who was coming to interview me about my progressive views on feminism and beauty. (The irony of having this conversation before that one was not lost on me.)

Julia, my fraternal twin sister, recently said, "We all have a different mirror." It was prescient: We'd been sitting around with Wallace, complaining about how beer makes us bloated, which was probably very rude as Wallace was drinking one. "I just don't know where you put it," I said, gesturing to her long, flat tummy. One beer and my stomach puffs up in protest, but Wallace's body is always the same size. She said, "It goes to the back of my legs," and Julia and I could barely contain our skepticism: Wallace's legs, like the rest of her, are slender and long. Julia's mirror comment made us all laugh.

"It's so true," I said, gleeful to bond over dysmorphia. "When I look in the mirror, I see the Michelin Man!"

"Oh, I've seen him in mine before, too," said Julia, who is—like my aforementioned college friend—someone I loom over.

Despite our difference in height and weight, my sister and I have grown into the same shape, which has magnified for me the remarkable difference in how we view ourselves and each other. We once tried on the same pair of leather pants, and they stretched identically across our stomachs, each of us insisting that the pants looked great on the other one and awful on us. I could see that they were pulling on us in the same way; I loved the way the material clung to her—I thought it looked sexy, and I was jealous. We both bought the pants and then admitted to each other years later that we got rid of them shortly thereafter.

A so-called good feminist in today's world thinks that bodies in their natural state—cellulite, rolls, stretch marks, and all—are perfect. It's almost like someone forgot to tell us to include ourselves. Or maybe we're so used to hating the things that we're suddenly supposed to celebrate that it's simply easier to start with everyone else. For decades, women's media discussed our appearance as a problem to be solved, with fashion and beauty being the solution. It's a simple formula: tell the reader they are doing something wrong, dangle a solution to an issue they didn't realize they had, make them feel just inferior enough to need an article, and then a product, to fix them. And in the alleged digital feminist revolution of the early 2010s, there was a new layer: insist that the readers are perfect while you make them feel broken. Call them badass babes and then tell them what jeans will flatter their tummies. It was the same old story, just packaged differently.

Now, though, the stories readers click on the most are the ones that subvert that oh-so-privileged thin/white/straight/cisgender identity. And in fact, the most popular image from my last New York Fashion Week at *Nylon* was a photo of a black woman with a bedazzled prosthetic leg. It got over six thousand likes within two hours. Young women are so supportive of other people's differences that I get the chills thinking about it. No matter where my career takes me, my plan is to inundate the world with beautiful differences to celebrate until we all have the strength to turn that support inward, or until it just seeps in like osmosis, counteracting everything we've previously absorbed and accepted as true.

6

Happy Weight

Like most millennials and Gen Zers, I was taught growing up that commercial beauty standards aren't realistic. We learned in class about how magazines intentionally altered photos of women, and about the ways the advertising industry lied to us regarding what people should look like in order to incentivize us to spend money. In high school I remember wanting to buy a shirt that said "Fuck Your Beauty Standards," but my mom wouldn't let me, not because of the sentiment but because of the word "fuck." That is to say that I am part of a generation that is well versed in the language of the beauty myth, in the idea that Western feminine beauty ideals rest heavily on hetero-normativity, sexism, racism, and misogyny, and that these ideals attempt to distract women with an obsession over our appearances so that we remain second-class citizens. But when it comes to our own lives and what we say to ourselves when no one else is listening, we all still have a long way to go. To paraphrase what one friend said to me—a woman who has a very successful career in finance—we know beauty is a myth, but we still subscribe to it. And another, a queer writer known for brilliant feminist hot takes, said to me that she understands and supports body positivity but only as it applies to other people.

It's as though the intellectualizing of body politics isn't enough to conquer the dominant cultural messaging we're constantly barraged with. It's especially not enough when that messaging is validated by real-life personal experiences—like how people talk to you about your body, like the love you receive. It's one thing to objectively understand that your value is independent of how thin you are, but when people around you still struggle to disentangle thinness from attractiveness, it's hard to keep in mind.

In few instances is this more apparent than when we date: there is an urgency to be skinny and fit when single, which is quickly abandoned once a relationship is defined. Just about everyone, myself included, gains weight at the beginning of a relationship. The phenomenon has been fully studied and documented, and a quick google of "happy weight" or "relationship weight" gives you not just a definition but tons and tons of tips for how to avoid it. For me, though, putting on pounds wasn't just a happy nuisance. It was the fact that I lost weight to get in a relationship in the first place that got me in trouble.

When you go hungry, you're telling yourself, simply, that your body doesn't need food to survive, but the drive to do so is indicative of something larger. In many ways, an eating disorder, or compulsive dieting, or whatever you want to call it, is a metaphor for a suppression of emotional needs, too. Thinness, then, was idealized for me because it represented *not* having needs—not just nutritional ones but the need for support from other people. As someone who has always been obsessed with the idea of being totally independent, this, in a twisted way, was the embodiment of what I thought the shape of my life was supposed to be.

It makes a lot of sense when you think about the version of the self that people try to present during courtship: for many, the most attractive others are the ones who appear to need the least from us, which is ultimately a projection about what *we* might need from *them*. For a long time, I was afraid to need anything from anyone—so I picked people who had nothing to give me, anyway. I've seen my friends do this, too. And how many times have you reined in your own neediness in the beginning so as not to scare someone away? As women there is so much pressure to appear chill, to not catch feelings too soon. Then once you lock it down, it's safe to express what you need—and, if we're to continue the metaphor, safe to eat enough. We gain weight in the comfort of a defined relationship, trusting that under those circumstances we can express our full spectrum of needs without scaring someone off.

A lot of straight women I've talked to about happy weight are under the assumption that this isn't a problem for queer women—that a woman wouldn't need to try to be skinny to be more attractive to other women. There's a certain amount of cultural fantasy about what it's like when there are no men around, as though we exist in a vacuum. If only!

My senior year of college, when I was fully immersed in a bubble of queer body positivity, I developed a major crush on my boss at Babeland. It had been a few years since I came out, and I'd gained back the weight I'd lost the summer that I started dating Lucy. But despite the activist circle I was running around in, I felt my own shape was bad, and wrong, and I was desperate for her to like me back despite what I saw as my flaws. So falling for her at twenty-one was the gym every day, no carbs / no dairy until she was in my bed. Her name was Avery, and she was twenty-eight. Once she loved me all that effort was quickly replaced by potato chips standing up in the kitchen; vegan chili spooning on the couch; beer sitting on the floor. We talked for hours and snacked on salty things, and the hip bones she'd grabbed on to so tightly started to fade into surprising new pillows perched at my sides. The calculated discipline of constant, mild hunger and sore muscles took a back seat to the magic urgency of the present. It was such a relief.

Despite our age difference we had a lot in common: radical politics, a love of feminist punk music, earnest enthusiasm for community activism, bad jokes. She met my family and got along with them instantly. Over the next two semesters she gradually moved in with me, and I was the happiest I'd ever been.

Despite my internship, my prospects for employment were looking pretty grim. I'd applied to over fifty different editorial assistant jobs and didn't hear back from any of them until someone wrote to me and said, "Sweetie, there's a typo in your resume." I was equal parts ambitious and underqualified. I was even turned down for the office manager position that had opened up where I was interning. Finally, it turned out that one of the Feminist Press's authors, who ran an online magazine about women's issues in the basement of the abortion clinic she owned, was looking for an editorial assistant, and I got the job.

The day before I graduated, my grandma—my dad's mom—died. By that point she'd had Alzheimer's for about ten years, and the illness had made her into the sweet old lady she never was when I was growing up. (I first learned about the Holocaust, and survivors, as a kid from my parents as justification for why she said such bizarrely hurtful things to me, like telling me I was ugly to "ward off the evil eye.") But with dementia she was all high-pitched giggles and childlike wonder—her greatest crime was wandering into a neighbor's yard to pick flowers. She'd descend into frustrated confusion, but the meanness was gone, as though without her memories there wasn't anything to be angry about.

Both my grandparents had been in a nursing home in Boston, about four hours north of where they'd lived in Forest Hills,

Queens. They went there a few years after my grandmother got sick because my grandfather, who was going blind, tried to kill himself (he'd lost his sight, she'd lost her mind, "What was there to live for?"). They'd kept their house, though, and when she died that spring, it was empty. It was perfect, if morbid, timing: I wasn't sure how I'd be able to live in the city on my new starter-job wages. My grandparents' old house seemed like the perfect solution. My two sisters soon also decided to move in. My parents were happy we'd all be together, and my grandfather was thrilled. He didn't know I was bringing a girlfriend. At this point he was still asking me why I never had a boyfriend, and my consistent reply was, "What do I need a boyfriend for?"

We were extremely privileged to have the opportunity to live in NYC so cheaply. The expenses of the house were equivalent to sharing a tiny room in Bushwick (NYC was very different in 2011), but it was *a house*, in a quiet neighborhood, with my sisters and girlfriend instead of strangers as roommates. Living there right after college is one of the reasons why I was able to spend a few years in assistant roles and freelance writing without taking a side job in the service industry like many people have to do. Entry-level publishing jobs at that point did not pay enough to support a comfortable life in New York without another job or other financial support (I have to assume that most people are on their parents' payroll while making certain salaries and living in certain neighborhoods, or they have spousal support), which means people who make it in the industry usually come from a certain economic class. It's gotten better—entry-level jobs where I work now pay nearly twice what they did when I was starting out. It's still not enough to be super comfortable, but it's enough to get by. If we hadn't been able to live there, I'm not sure if I would have become an editor at all.

So we all moved in, and Avery and I adopted a dog from a local rescue, an elderly five-pound poodle/bichon mix with a sweet little lopsided trot. We named her Kimberly. We were pretty far away from the city and all of our friends, but we were set up for domestic bliss. I had had other girlfriends before—many—but this was the first time I really understood the difference between dating and a serious relationship. It wasn't just that we did everything together; our lives became intertwined.

She wanted to get married and have kids, but I insisted I was too young. Even though I was planning on spending the rest of my life with her, I knew there was something inappropriate about getting married right out of college. Gay marriage wasn't legal yet, anyway, which I was secretly relieved about. It was a built-in reason to put it off. On her thirtieth birthday we got a domestic partnership as a compromise. I wore a short purple lace dress to the courthouse, and Julia took iPhone photos of us in the driveway when we returned. In the photos, we're holding both Kimberly and the partnership certificate.

A lot of really wonderful things happened in our partnership. We took trips to new places, we worked together to rehabilitate Kimberly, and we continued to do activism together, organizing the NYC Dyke March and hosting events at our house. We had our own private relationship language, things no one else would understand. We supported each other through deaths on both sides of our families. We were best friends.

And for a while, that was enough for me. But . . . I was so young when we started dating. I'd overestimated my readiness for something so serious, mistaking my college escapades for actual experience. Meanwhile, she'd had her entire twenties to date people and figure out what she wanted and needed. I had no idea on either front.

Because of the age difference, our friends were all in different life places, too, and we spent summers going to her friends' weddings and then, soon after, baby showers. I was welcomed into these major life events with open arms, but the result was that I never really got to feel like I was in my early twenties. I never got to be directionless, or question my own future. I felt pressure to know what I wanted from life, when the truth was that I had no idea. I was pretending to be on par with people in their early thirties, which in hindsight I so clearly wasn't. While my peers were out getting wasted and making mistakes, I was meeting babies. I was growing resentful without realizing why.

I also had this feeling like we were perpetually just waiting for the next hard thing to pass before we could enjoy our lives. She just needed to quit her job or start a new one or go back to school or get past someone's stressful wedding or funeral; we just needed to move or get a new car or go on vacation, and then after that we could be happy. At some point I realized the common denominator wasn't the events themselves, but the way we were approaching them: there was always *something* on the horizon preventing us from being able to be okay, and once that event happened, there would be another. I was hardly ever in the moment. We were living for a future that would never come to fruition.

But the thing that broke me was that she stopped wanting to be physically intimate. No reason fully articulated but that she just didn't want to. When I tried to talk to her about it, she reacted with defensiveness and would lash out. I was already coming from such a hurt place in these confrontations that it was easy for her to make me cry. She told me that my disappointment about sex stressed her out and made her want to do it even less. I wondered if maybe it was an age-difference thing, and I also wondered if maybe I was just deeply unattractive.

I needed to be intimate to feel connected to her, but there was no room to express it. So as a frantic solution I stopped eating meals again, as though I didn't need anything at all. I went to bed earlier and earlier, usually alone. My stomach flattened out again, legs became insect-like, even elbows became somehow sharper. I was hungry for her affection but also for my own sense of joy and fulfillment. I tried to re-create the manic thinness of our courtship, when the air was so heavy with sexual tension I *couldn't* eat. It didn't make a difference, but it was something I could control, unlike her desire for me, which I didn't realize actually had nothing to do with the shape of my body.

Once, I told her that I'd given up carbs so she'd be attracted to me again, and she told me not to blame that behavior on her. We'd never talked about my fluctuating weight before.

"Don't you think it's problematic that you need sex to feel good about yourself?" she said another time, not really a question but an accusation. All our communication about the issue started to take the same shape. I'd pretend to not need anything and hold my feelings in until I couldn't anymore, and then I'd blurt something out; she'd say I was being dramatic or something else hurtful and unrelated; I'd cry; she'd get annoyed at me for crying. This went on for years. It didn't occur to me to leave. I simply thought, *This is what my life is going to be*.

In early 2013 I started working at Refinery29 and suddenly had a very demanding job with which to busy myself. My commute from Forest Hills to downtown Manhattan was about an hour and a half, so I was rarely home. I was grateful for the long hours and the work I'd usually always need to finish up at home; it was a welcome distraction and I threw myself into it completely.

I knew that Avery was proud of my success and admired me for it, but it was also a source of tension; she was going back to school to finish her degree in economics, so our lives started going in very different directions. When I went to *Nylon* a year and a half later, my schedule filled up even more with networking events, and that created further conflict: during one terrible fight in particular she revealed a worry that I'd rather do drugs with my "new *Nylon* friends" than spend time with her. (For the record, I've never done anything like that, but it was indicative of her worst fears about what my life was turning into—and maybe a reflection of how distant I was being. In the blank space where open communication should have been, it was easy to think the worst.)

Four years after we moved into his old house, my grandfather died, and our relationship was dying, too. We'd lost the ability to communicate with each other, and I felt completely and totally alone, even though we shared space and friends and had become like family. My older sister's boyfriend drove the four of us up to Boston for the funeral. In the back seat Avery squeezed my hand and with a face full of tears she whispered, "Try to remember that you love me, okay?"

Driving back from his memorial service in a torrential downpour, we got rear-ended on the highway. My neck snapped backward and forward, and I had the feeling I was being jolted awake from a deep sleep. I reentered my body as the car leapt forward, suddenly aware of the pain I'd been ignoring, no longer able to hide from it.

Most women grow up learning that real relationships are hard. But for me that mantra had become an excuse to remain unhappy. Love takes work, but we weren't doing the work required to maintain a long-term relationship. We were avoiding it, until the issues got bigger and bigger. Sex, of course, wasn't the real issue but a symptom of a larger incompatibility, and I'd let my resentment become like a third person in the room. It was turning me into someone I hated: mean, impatient, withholding. I had felt so sad for so long that it became unsustainable and was replaced by anger and numbness. I felt no motivation to try to save the relationship. It was over.

I was twenty-six. We broke up a few months later, at the end of August, just before our five-year anniversary. She claimed to have had no idea how unhappy I was, and saying the words felt like having to amputate my own arm. It was the only thing left to do in order to save myself, and I knew in time I'd heal, but it was so painful. We decided to share custody of Kimberly, loosely agreeing to trade her off every few weeks. On top of breaking up with her, I wasn't about to take her dog away from her, too.

Avery moved out first while I sat in the park with two friends, drinking bodega beer. I picked at the grass, felt its dampness through my jeans.

"I need to be single for the rest of my twenties," I told them, while they rolled their eyes. Later, when the park was spinning, my friend Christina downloaded Tinder on my phone and we looked at cute girls while I marveled at how many people had been out there all along.

"Maybe actually I need to fuck all of them," I said, a slurred change of heart.

"That's more like it," Christina replied approvingly. I was nearly seeing double from the beer and the heat.

When I started seeing Avery, dating apps didn't exist. We'd met in person, at work, and I still had a flip phone. By the end of our relationship I'd been having a recurring dream about using Tinder for months. That night I swiped madly from my bed, falling asleep with my phone in my hand. During the breakup I had been convinced that I wanted to be alone, but suddenly all I could think about was meeting someone. It wasn't really solitude I'd been craving; in a lot of ways, I'd had that. I spent the first half of my twenties feeling rejected by the person I was in love with, and even though I was angry at her for it, I was mostly directing that anger inward, convinced that there was something unlovable about me. What I wanted was to be proven wrong by a successful relationship; I wanted real connection, and physical intimacy, and someone who had similar goals to mine who could challenge me in new ways and also cherish me at the end of my long, brutally stressful workdays. I woke up to several matches; the first was a girl who I'd known in high school. We went on a drinks date that week and then a second date that weekend to a party, after which she came home with me and spent the night. She was a (also, the aforementioned) Scorpio, a fact she told me while rolling her eyes. She was funny and tall, with short, floppy brown hair and doll-like blue eyes, and I could feel how much she liked me, but I had a phone full of potential and half a decade of unresolved feelings to wade through. I tried to let her down honestly with a text about how it was too close to my breakup for me to consider anything serious.

I went back to my Tinder deep dive. A few days later I swiped and swiped until I landed on a profile with blurry but artful photos. Her bio was a line from a poem. I thought, *This person is a red flag*. We matched immediately.

She messaged me quickly: "Can I borrow that jacket?" I said no. A day of anxious banter and then I asked her out, to which she said, "Please."

We met at a dark, trendy bar. She said her coworkers had told her she was dressed like Justin Timberlake, and she was: shiny black blazer over a T-shirt; short, curly bleached-blonde hair; slouchy pants rolled up at the ankle, sneakers. Over cocktails she told me she was a double Gemini and said, "Sorry in advance," with a dangerous smirk. Hours later, making out on the sidewalk at two a.m., she pushed me into a fence, thumbs carving into my ribs, and I felt like I was twenty again, or at least like my body was, or at least like if I was my skinniest self maybe I could make up for all the years I spent feeling like someone's creepy roommate instead of someone's girlfriend. Finally I untangled myself and took a cab home, crawling into bed around five a.m. and sleeping until noon. I awoke to a text from her, and from that moment on we were rarely out of contact.

I moved out of the house in Queens about a week later, packing my delicate things in canvas tote bags and the rest of my stuff in black garbage bags. Avery and I had lived together in a quiet, family-oriented neighborhood, but I had dreams of noisy, bustling Brooklyn, where life seemed more vibrant, more filled with possibility. Mimi, who I'd met as an intern at the Lesbian Herstory Archives in college, lived in Bed-Stuy, and for years I'd drive or take the bus to her brownstone-lined street. I was so envious of her cool Brooklyn babe life—friends within walking distance, dimly lit restaurants and bars, cute queer people of all kinds holding hands—and for a long time I didn't think I'd get to have something similar. But her partner, Rae, was opening a coffee shop two blocks from their home, and she put me in touch with the shop's landlord, who happened to have a studio apartment open in the same building. I was aching to live alone, but also scared, and living near my friends while also in my own space was the ideal situation. I felt that I couldn't fully grow up until I had my own little world to retreat to, that I was solely responsible for.

I didn't have a lot of belongings besides clothes and beauty products, which was for the best, since the studio I was moving into had enough room for my bed, a dresser, and a small couch; there was no closet, and only a tiny kitchenette. I ordered two clothing racks on Amazon and set them up in the corner of the living room / bedroom, and then overloaded them with clothes to the point where the racks were permanently leaning to one side. A few times they totally collapsed on me while I got dressed for work.

The studio was on the second floor, overlooking a busy street, with wide-set window ledges that I could sit in and look out at the community garden, which had a huge weeping willow tree next to a permanently parked, burnt-out orange car. I could hear music from the barbershop below, birds from the tree across the street, and the regular rumble of the G train beneath the building. I'd frequently see my friends walking by and could talk to them from my window. I'd never felt so proud.

I had a very specific vision for my first solo apartment, and it involved shining white walls, midcentury modern furniture with cozy gray accents, and a few well-placed, thriving succulents. Maybe a blush-pink throw would be draped just so over a Scandinavian sofa, and natural light would spill across the room, creating an elegant, ever-changing pattern that would dance across the hardwood floors. I'd purge my closet and reorganize it by color (black and white). Everything West Elm, nothing IKEA. My bed would always be made with sheets that were always clean. I wouldn't necessarily go full Marie Kondo, but I somehow wouldn't have to—my taste, when not compromised by roommates or a live-in partner—would lend itself to pristine minimalism.

Enter the actual things I filled said apartment with: two mismatched moody-red Persian rugs from Craigslist, an antique brass standing lamp with a rose stained-glass lampshade, a dresser hand-painted with flowers my mom got at a flea market twenty years ago, mismatched cups, five throw blankets of vastly different patterns and materials, an art collection that included a vintage painting of a poodle wearing sunglasses as well as an illustrated portrait of Hillary Clinton, and so, so many books about feminism and also aliens. The one thing I bought from West Elm was not the simple wooden coffee table of my daydreams but a very large, dark-blue velvet tufted couch, on which I placed a sheepskin. It sat surrounded by crystals, more lamps, several different things to smoke out of, a vintage wooden coffee table that I painted matte black, and a sculptural side table made of dark mirrors.

The farther into the corners of the space my crap went, the more it felt like mine. And there's a special thing that happens when you're surrounded only by your own belongings: your emotional stuff surrounds you, too, without distraction. There was suddenly nowhere to hide from my own self.

I invited the Gemini to come over the night I moved in. She showed up with a bottle of prosecco. I wish I could have let myself have that night alone; in hindsight, it would have been so important to know that I could be okay by myself. But I wasn't thinking about myself like that; I was just excited to see her.

Perhaps because I still had never actually been on my own, it was easy to quickly start spending most nights of the week together. My friends regarded the situation with skepticism. Eyebrows rose at me as I gushed about her. No one wanted to say the word "rebound," but I could basically hear them thinking it.

Time spent with her was never predictable. She wanted to look at the full-moon eclipse on my roof, drinking champagne from the bottle. She wanted to order takeout in our pajamas on Saturday nights, and in the middle of the week she convinced me to get out of bed at midnight to meet all her friends at a bar. She managed to sidestep confirming whether or not she was dating other people but always wanted to hold my hand in public. She checked a lot of superficial boxes: She was successful in a creative field that overlapped with mine. She had a beautiful apartment and stylish clothes. She loved to read books and go shopping. I was a nervous wreck.

It's so easy to think someone cares about you because she wants you—especially if you're not used to that kind of attention. But in the weeks and then months that followed, we never talked about love or tried to define our situation, though we'd frequently, teasingly ask each other, "So what are you looking for?" and take turns avoiding actually answering. I didn't think I could tell her that I wanted her to be my girlfriend—those words seemed so far away. It was hard to picture a formal commitment from her even though we were spending all our free time together. And I wasn't even sure I wanted that; everything during that time felt so raw and painful, like I was walking around inside out, experiencing the world for the first time, and it was hard to parse out what I thought I wanted from what I truly needed. When we weren't together, I was so anxious about what we were doing or not doing that food was just a memory of something I used to want. I got thinner and thinner. My breakup weight became my dating weight. But what I was hungry for shifted.

Meanwhile, I was navigating an every-other-week custody schedule with Avery and our poor old pup. It was a bumpy process, complicated further by the fact that we had broken up without fully working through our feelings together. There was still so much residual anger between us that little things like timing misunderstandings sparked heated conflict where we'd both yell. I also made the poor decision to write an article about my new single life ("The Newly Single Girl's Guide to Beauty," about trying to make time for aesthetic self-care when you're suddenly busy dating for the first time in a while—it was a bit of an exaggeration, since I was only dating one person), which turned out to be one of the most popular things I'd ever written—and she'd read it. The next time we spoke, after a miscommunication about when she was supposed to pick Kimberly up, she screamed into the phone, "Go back to your dates and your makeup," and hung up.

One morning in November, after three months of dating, I woke up in the Gemini's bed freezing. Her heat was broken. It turned off in the night, and as long as I knew her it never fully came back.

My clothes were in a frigid tangle on the floor, and even once I was fully dressed I was still cold. I was about to walk a chilly mile home to Bed-Stuy so I could get ready for work in my own apartment. I grabbed the first warm thing I saw from her permanent pile of unfolded clothes: a hoodie. I perched on the edge of her bed and said, "It's so cold. Can I wear this home?"

"Please," she said.

Her hoodie was thick and black and very expensive. I wore

it under my leather jacket, touched the edges of the sleeves with my ice-cold fingertips as I floated home, marveling at the changing leaves like I'd never seen autumn before.

I didn't give it back, not yet. It was so warm, and when we were apart, something was starting to feel so cold. Once, it took her a full day to text me back, so I wore it around my apartment while I paced. In hindsight, this dynamic was probably exactly what I needed: I absolutely was not ready for a relationship, and all the signs were there that she didn't want one. But having never dated as an adult was a handicap; my only references other than my very recent serious relationship were from college. The pace was stressful and foreign.

A few weeks later I asked if I could take her hoodie with me on a business trip to Minnesota. "Of course," she said. "It's great for airplanes." She traveled a lot, too, and it turned out we were going to be gone for the same period of time. We saw each other the night we both returned. I burst into her apartment and tackled her onto her couch. We ordered Chinese food and ate it on the floor. But she fell asleep with all her clothes on, on top of the covers, and the next time she left the city she didn't tell me when she got back.

"She just has this vibe like she could break my heart at any second," I told a work friend, trying to describe the baseline anxiety I'd started to feel. "If you feel like that now, she already has," he replied.

And sure enough, in December, she stopped wanting to

be around me. After we suddenly went a whole week without seeing each other, I tried to talk to her about it and did a terrible job; she said she felt like I was just comparing her to Avery instead of listening. In turn, I felt like she was withdrawing because I'd started to need more from her, the antithesis to how I'd originally presented myself. As for how quickly she'd gone from texting me all day and trying to see me almost every night to radio silence, she said, abruptly, "I'm not trying to dive into a relationship with someone who just got out of one."

"I didn't realize you were holding that against me," I said, trying not to cry.

She folded her arms over her chest, becoming a tiny, defiant ball in the corner of my couch, and said nothing.

Throughout that fall, the Scorpio had never really given up on me, despite how clearly I'd rejected her. We'd seen each other for dinner every few weeks, texting occasionally, but I'd kept her at arm's length, afraid of how serious I sensed she wanted to be. When the Gemini turned from hot to cold, though, and wouldn't have a real conversation with me about it, I went on a few dates with someone a friend had set me up with, and then I started seeing the Scorpio regularly. Her persistence and patience had become very attractive.

As I processed the situation with my sister Miriam, she

said, "You know, how someone treats you is the most important thing about them." My mind was blown. It hadn't even occurred to me that how someone treated me could factor into my assessment of them at all.

And, as much as I'd yearned for it, I couldn't stand to be alone in my apartment. I'd get stuck staring in the mirror, zeroing in on the way my stomach stuck out, overcome with shame. So I made sure I was never alone. It was like Avery had cursed me: "Don't you think it's problematic that you need sex to feel good about yourself?" she'd said. And it was.

Right in the middle of all of this, my mom was diagnosed with breast cancer. She called me at work to tell me; I took the call in the hallway because I didn't have anywhere else to be alone. I sat on the floor and cried into the phone. When we hung up, I texted Leila to come out and talk to me, but we both knew there was nothing she could say to make me feel better, so I decided to go home. On the subway I texted the Gemini, who didn't respond. She called me later that night, and we made plans to get breakfast before I headed out to Long Island to be with my family for the weekend; but in the morning she cancelled, saying a work situation had come up.

During my final text exchange with the Gemini, I was in the hospital waiting room with my sisters and my dad while my mom had surgery. Without any closure she suddenly just stopped writing me back. My heart felt like it was breaking, but I wasn't sure what or who it was breaking for. Myself, I guess.

Meanwhile, my mom made a full recovery. That was the good news—the best and most important news ever, really. The bad news was that the reality of being on my own was finally starting to sink in, and I realized I had no idea how to be an adult. I'd never felt so alone or so incompetent. And then, in January, when I was in Utah for Sundance, my maternal grandfather died, the third of my grandparents to pass away in just a few short years. He and I had had a special bond, and when my mom called to tell me, I sunk into the Airbnb bed in sobs, cancelling my celebrity interviews for the rest of the week.

It felt like life was spinning out of control, but the more I spun out, the gentler the Scorpio was to me. Despite how many times I initially pushed her away, we ended up being together for just over a year. During that time I was promoted to digital director at *Nylon* and started making real money, most of which I spent with her: we ate out all the time, greasy comfort food like burgers and tacos; we'd drink beer and tequila and spend entire weekends in bed. I had a gushy short essay published in *Dope Girls*, a zine for women who enjoy cannabis, and it began, "In the tender, anxious space between the ease of *I like you* and the terrifying plunge of *I love you* we start to smoke weed together." I'd never laughed so much with anyone in my life.

Eventually, the skinniness that symbolized the unhappiness of the first half of my twenties dissolved, and I gained weight—a good amount. Enough to need new clothes. But I hadn't done any real emotional work around my relationship to my body. I had barely acknowledged it was an issue. So when suddenly my clothes didn't fit me, I was not at all ready to be okay with it.

As soon as I realized it was happening, I went into overdrive trying to course correct. It's never been hard for me to lose weight if I want to—what's hard is doing it moderately or slowly. I shed the pounds quickly but became depressed and anxious, always exhausted, needing to go to bed early. I developed dark circles under my eyes, and my hair thinned out. I stopped seeing my friends. Instead I started going to barre classes daily and became addicted to the endorphins; it was the only time of day I'd feel at peace. Eventually I got a bad cold, and it didn't go away. Every day I felt sicker and sicker but didn't connect it to how poorly I was taking care of myself. I stopped getting along with my family, which made everyone rightfully furious with me, and I had no explanation. I felt like the absolute worst person on earth.

This was a particularly pivotal moment in my career. The digital department of *Nylon* under me had become so successful that my title was changed from digital director to digital editor in chief in a matter of months, which caused a lot of conflict with the print editors—there was now an editor in chief of the magazine, and me, a deeply uncomfortable situation that had us inherently pitted against each other instead of collaborating. Our boss was interested in pushing me forward as the face of the brand, which meant I was starting to speak at conferences, represent the magazine at important events, and I was on camera all the time. I was chosen to host our first-ever premium news show, which would air on Amazon Prime. I started to actually get photographed by street style photographers instead of ignored. I was also starving, and suffering for it, but because of my work environment it felt justified; the correlation between my weight and my professional value felt very real. Even in hindsight I am fairly certain this wasn't just in my head, based on the biases of the person in charge of making my role so outward facing—a middle-aged straight white man—and the context of the industry.

My coworkers were commenting on my body constantly. I started wearing loose clothing to avoid my weight being a topic of conversation. At one point I got the stomach flu and was literally wasting away; a woman from the marketing department said to me, "Can you just breathe on me so I can catch it?"

Meanwhile, the Scorpio and I had started fighting all the time. We couldn't really talk about what was happening, so she tried to joke about it: "Remember when you got fat?" she frequently said in a baby voice, which just about drove me insane. There were many other issues at play—we wanted different things from life and each other—but everything was compounded into our fights about my eating and working out. As supportive as she'd been, she had no patience for what she couldn't fix or control. When she was annoyed, she became cruel.

I no longer wanted to go out at night with her (or anyone), and so she'd go to bars without me and then come to my apartment when the sun was rising, smelling like cigarettes and cheap beer. She said it was mean that I asked her to shower before getting in my bed, but the smell made my eyes water. On one such night she'd run into her most recent ex-girlfriend and told me that this woman had wept on the barstool next to her about how sad it was that they were no longer in love; she then pulled the Scorpio by the arm into the bathroom. They spent hours reminiscing together, wasted. Hearing this story, I became hysterical, and in response she told me it wasn't a big deal: girls were always pulling her into bathrooms, she said. She claimed to not understand how that made it even worse.

There were a thousand fights like this: a million sharp words, an arsenal of misunderstandings and poorly handled confrontations, a running tab of hurt feelings that never felt resolved no matter how direct I tried to be with her. Instead they piled on top of one another, making every incident feel worse than it was, painful parts of a whole that was clearly unsustainable.

When I finally told her I wanted to break up, it took weeks for her to hear me. She tried to tell me that my "mental illness" was making me push her away. She said the suddenness with which I wanted to end things was abusive. She said I didn't know how to love. She said a lot of really awful things, actually, and to this day sometimes I'll suddenly remember one of them and will feel angry and hurt all over again. Mostly I feel mad at myself for letting it drag on for so long. But that experience saved my life: she'd made me promise to tell my therapist that I was starving myself, and I agreed to it.

We finally broke up for good one day in the beginning of March, and early the very next morning I had to go to Austin, Texas, for South by Southwest (SXSW). I made it there but was barely functioning, going to the bare minimum of events and hiding in my hotel room. Lying on the scratchy Hilton couch in a bathrobe at noon, I ended up Gchatting with Avery. It had been almost two years since we'd broken up. I said, "How much the Scorpio and I processed our breakup made me realize how little you and I did."

She said, "We didn't at all. I talked to everyone but you about it."

I apologized for publishing "The Newly Single Girl's Guide to Beauty." I knew it had hurt her. She said, "You broke my heart, but I know I broke yours before that."

I told her how devastated I'd been that we stopped being physically intimate. She said, "Didn't you realize that that was about my own depression, and not about you?" Of course, I hadn't.

Alone in my hotel room, I cried and cried. It was like I had to leave New York in order to fully feel everything I'd been avoiding. I grieved every breakup I'd ever been through at once, mourning the losses of all the women who had moved in and out of my life, none of whom turned out to be the partners I needed but whom I'd cared for deeply anyway. I grieved for the years of my life I'd spent not speaking up for myself, years I'd never get the chance to do over.

The Scorpio and I talked on the phone a few days later, and I told her what the doctor had told me about my blood levels. She said, "I'm so angry at you for not dealing with this sooner." We didn't speak again.

That spring, even though I'd started treatment, I was about to hit my lowest weight ever: around one hundred pounds. In April I posted a photo on Instagram of myself at Coachella in a red floral dress, looking like I was about to drop dead; all the comments were compliments.

Mimi pointed out to me that the last time you play out a pattern is the worst time. And true to form after I stopped speaking to the Scorpio, I found myself in yet another intense romantic situation. This time it was like all the issues I'd had in other relationships—poor communication and toxic behavior all around—were put into an Instant Pot and pressure-cooked into one explosive rebound. Having learned at least a little lesson, I got myself out of that one within a few months. But I did it sloppily, once again starting to see someone new before the dust had fully settled. This newest person was Wallace, and I hated that she had to start dating me under those circumstances.

Wallace was so kind and well-adjusted, and there I was, a total mess in the wake of yet another breakup from an ill-advised relationship. I was filled with shame but also with self-awareness: it was like I was watching myself from above, going through the motions of the same old story that had held me hostage for years. I wanted out. But I also wanted Wallace, and I wanted to keep her.

She was my neighbor. From the moment I'd met her two years prior, at the coffee shop between our apartments right after I moved to Brooklyn, I thought she was just about the cutest thing I'd ever seen: long, curly brown ringlets framing an angular face, with huge green eyes and an easy grin, and long, slender limbs that were golden from the sun. She always wore ripped black jeans and soft band T-shirts and had full sleeve tattoos on both arms that featured both Sade and a scene from *Jaws*. She was a dog walker and a musician and an artist, bursting with contagious creative energy. She grew up in North Carolina, and words became softer in her mouth, stretched out luxuriously: "Orange" became *arnge*. "Chocolate" became *chahk-lit*. "Avocado" was *ah-vuh-cah-duh*. "Did you eat?" was rolled into one: *Didjaeat?* Or sometimes just, *Jeet?* She always smelled good, thanks to what I'd later learn was an extensive collection of designer fragrances.

We had mutual close friends, so we'd occasionally hung out in groups but had never been alone together. For years I had made sure that our friends knew about my crush, hoping that someday it might get back to her. I'd say little things when we were all together and she was out of earshot, like, "Imagine being Wallace's girlfriend."

It was early summer. She'd just gotten out of a long-term relationship and had started messaging me daily on social media. Eventually she gave me her number in an Instagram DM, and I texted her that I liked her before we even went on a date. She already knew, though—my plan had worked. She had told a mutual friend that she had a crush on me, and that friend grinned and said, "Gab has a crush on you, too." There was something very middle school dance about the whole thing. If I could have passed her a note in class saying, "Do you like me? Circle YES/NO," I would have.

She took me to see an indie musician I'd loved in high school, and sitting next to each other in the ornate concert hall, our elbows gingerly touched. On the subway back to Brooklyn, she blushed while she told me her birth chart. A week later, walking home from a bar on a night so foggy the air felt like soup, I wrapped my arms around her neck, and we kissed. By August she was my girlfriend.

This time was different, though. I was totally crazy about her, and at the same time it was the least crazy I'd ever felt. I knew that if I was going to be a good partner to her, long-term, I had a lot of work to do, and for the first time in my life I had the inner resources to actually do the work. For my entire twenties, I had been in back-to-back relationships without ever taking a minute to think about what I really needed. I desperately wanted to break my habit of one relationship bleeding into the next, of not saying what I needed, of leaning on weight loss as a distraction. It was too destructive, to me and to anyone who made the mistake of getting involved with me.

I was texting my nutritionist pictures of my meals and seeing my therapist twice a week. I told Wallace about it, and she reacted with kindness and support, but she followed my lead, not bringing it up unless I did. I wanted her to know everything about me, but I didn't want her to ever have to experience the darker parts. It's hard to be radically honest about things that you're ashamed of. I felt like it sounded whiny and superficial. But she never once judged me or got mad at me.

In September 2017, when we'd been dating for just a couple of months, right in the middle of New York Fashion Week, *Nylon*'s print magazine shut down. Suddenly I was editor in chief of an all-digital media company. This was the first NYFW that I wasn't starving myself for, and I was walking a tightrope to prevent myself from descending into self-loathing as I tried to squeeze into borrowed samples and posed nervously for street style photographers. When you start eating regularly after a period of starvation, usually your stomach is the first to show it since your ab muscles have broken down, and I was so self-conscious about my new little belly. Looking back at pictures now, it's not visible, but I wouldn't have believed that at the time.

When news of the magazine folding and the layoffs hit the press, there was extra attention on me, attention I wasn't prepared for. *Nylon* print had been a beloved magazine with fashion editors who knew everyone in the industry, and even though I had nothing to do with the decision to go all digital, there was a certain level of blame I absorbed since I was taking over as EIC (rather than, I don't know, quitting in protest? I'm not sure how I was expected to handle the situation. I loved my job. I also needed it). There were awkward conversations with PR people, sidelong glances directed at me in the front row at fashion shows, and a barrage of social media outrage to navigate. I felt horrible for my colleagues who were laid off and at the same time felt extremely lucky to still have a regular paycheck in such a tumultuous media landscape, a survivor's guilt that I didn't know what to do with. Any other year it would have been a great excuse to stop eating altogether. It was terrible timing psychologically, but I made it through, making a point to eat lunch every single day, to carry snacks in my bag. I felt awful for focusing on what felt like such a vapid thing while people had lost their jobs, but I also was finally understanding that my disordered eating was about so much more than how I looked.

Toward the end of the week, I brought Wallace with me to a Tiffany's fragrance party where St. Vincent performed on a small stage in a skintight red leather frock and piles of diamonds draped on her pale skin. I wore a long, silvery silk Tibi dress with a black lace turtleneck underneath. It was tighter than I expected, clinging to the new shape of my body. On my way there an older woman stopped me on the street and said, "Honey, you look amazing." She was a total stranger who had no reason to be nice to me. I wanted to hug her.

One morning in October we were lying quietly on my bed; Wallace was spooning me, the warmth of her torso pressing into my back, early golden light from outside illuminating the soft arm hairs on her forearms, which were still tan from the summer. She said, "You know I love you, right?"

"You know I love you, too," I replied, not a question.

We had Thanksgiving with her mom, and I ate ham biscuits for the first time. After Christmas I went with her to her hometown in North Carolina. We spent winter bundled in blankets. In the spring, for my twenty-ninth birthday, we went to Paris, and then Amsterdam. And in the fall, a year and a half after our first date, she moved in. We obsessed over hanging her art alongside mine, delighting in the commingling of our belongings. And then, eventually, it became abundantly clear that my little Bed-Stuy apartment—which had been perfect for me—wasn't big enough for the life we were making together, and we found a new one.

I hit the target weight set for me by my doctor. When my tiny clothes stopped fitting, I got rid of them. I've never tried to change my body to be more lovable for her; and, maybe more importantly, I've never pretended to not need things from her. It's not perfect: Sometimes it takes me days to articulate a feeling. Some days every meal feels like a choice I have to make. Sometimes I can't help but complain about how different my body feels from when we first started dating. She says, "But you were a tiny twig," and covers me in kisses.

Driving back from her family's Christmas in 2018, a ten-to-twelve-hour drive, we listened to Michelle Obama's beautiful memoir, *Becoming*. I was struck by the depth and nuance with which she described her marriage, the kind of understanding that comes after decades of emotional labor. I don't claim to have that sort of insight into what makes our love work—not yet. I know we still have so much to discover about each other. But the foundation we've laid since our first kiss in the summer of 2017 is stronger than anything I've experienced. It's more honest, and it's gentler, and it's built on compassion rather than expectation.

Looking back at the patterns of my relationships in my twenties, the association between my weight and my happiness is embarrassingly obvious: I'm heaviest when I'm happy. This is true for most women I know. Happy weight happens when you're in love and you stop worrying so much about how good you look because you're so distracted by how good you *feel*. Objectively it's wonderful. And yet it has terrible connotations. It signifies that you've let yourself go. God forbid.

I think the key for me has been not necessarily "letting myself go" but letting go of the things that are holding me back—like the idea that if you pretend to not have needs, the needs will go away. They don't, of course; needs that you put on hold just show up disguised as other needs. Staying in relationships that weren't making me happy wasn't serving me, nor was trying to control my weight. I'm my best self right now, several sizes up from what I used to consider my best-*looking* self.

Again and again, so many of us make the mistake of

thinking that how thin we are is indicative of how deserving of love we are. Thinness—because of the way it's still sexualized and glorified in pop culture—becomes synonymous with desirability, even if we know objectively that it's oppressive. Even if we would never stand for someone talking to our best friend the way we talk to ourselves.

In reality, the kind of thinness we're used to seeing usually comes with a price. For me, that price was my health and my relationships. I learned the hard way that it's happy weight, and everything that comes with it, that's aspirational. It's built in to the phrase itself. I just didn't know it until I got here.

7

Fashion Weak

I set the fire alarm off at my first New York Fashion Week. It was 2013 and I was backstage at one of the bigger shows. I was, in fact, doing solely backstage beauty reporting at the time and had waited about two hours in what appeared to be a dimly lit airplane hangar while PR people clad in all black clutched clipboards and murmured anxiously into headsets. All the beauty editors had received one-sheets (a page-long overview of the hair, makeup, and nails for the show) so we knew that, like many shows that season, it would be "no-makeup makeup" and simple, middle-parted hair. In short, for beauty reporting, it was a big to-do for nothing. We all waited around, though, because the lead hairstylist and makeup artist were well-known names, and a quote from them could become an entire story.

I had several more backstages to run to, and so when two

hours had passed and neither the models nor the glam teams had emerged, I decided to call it. But when I tried to leave, the main door was being blocked by security. Just over the security guard's shoulders I could see the models doing a run-through in the hallway. So I retreated backstage and noticed that at the back of the hangar, all the way in the dark, there was the glowing outline of another exit. I snuck over to it and pushed the door open. It opened to nothing—there was a three-foot drop and then the river.

That's when the alarm sounded, blaring throughout the backstage area. Immediately, two very butch female security guards appeared, and—I'm not proud of this—I burst into tears. "I'm just trying to leave," I said. They responded with some barely concealed sighs and offered to help me to the front exit. They walked on either side of me, slightly behind, and we pushed past the line of models until I got to the exit. When I took a step outside and the door immediately closed behind me, I realized that I hadn't really been helped out—I'd been kicked out.

I quickly learned that just about everybody has a first NYFW horror story. One of my editors comforted me with a story about the time she'd accidentally leaned on a button that opened a garage door, which happened to be serving as the backdrop for the runway, and instead of playing it cool, she ducked out of the space as the door rose. Those without horror stories had, at the very least, warnings: Don't take anything personally. Don't compare yourself to the models. Don't wear new shoes. Don't cry until you get home.

I always thought that I liked fashion, but really, I liked *clothes*. Fashion is a different beast entirely, and it's a culture that hinges on something impossible to maintain: exclusivity. I had no idea what I was getting into.

Since I started out as a beauty editor, I was eased into the fashion world. My first few times at New York Fashion Week were spent doing backstage reporting, which means you dash from venue to venue several hours before the shows start. It's a lot of arduous interviews (depending, I guess, on how excited you are to hear about bold brows and dewy skin on repeat) and a lot of running around, but in general it was pretty low stakes: backstage you could wear whatever you wanted, as long as you didn't get in anyone's way. And people who worked in beauty were generally nice—I found there's a kind of nurturing personality that's attracted to doing hair, nails, and makeup. Certain manicurists were known to do editors' nails during preshow interviews. Everyone knew everyone. I didn't mind missing out on the actual shows. I wasn't that interested in them. I wanted to know about makeup and hair tricks that people could actually use, rather than clothes that I couldn't afford.

I started actually attending shows when I went to *Nylon* in 2014 as a senior editor, and it didn't take me long to realize that despite what it looks like on Instagram, very few people actually enjoy Fashion Week (fashion *month* if you work for a company with enough money to send you to the European shows). And really, for people who are there to work, what's to enjoy? The days of "the tents"—when NYFW had one sponsor and so all the shows happened in one place—ended shortly after I started working in fashion, so there were only one or two seasons when I got to experience that luxury. The weeklong event that I came up in was spread throughout Manhattan, and Brooklyn too, with multiple conflicting calendars making it impossible to be anywhere on time. It was chaotic, zoo-like—and the worst part was that you were expected to look perfect, so even though it involved quite literally running around the city, when you hit the corner filled with street style photographers or you took your seat next to a former boss, not a single hair could be out of place.

Fashion Week in general is the last remaining vestige of a dying ethos. On a superficial, capitalistic level, it's totally at odds with what we know about contemporary consumer behavior: In our digital age people want instant gratification, especially when it comes to fashion. But aside from the few brands that have recently shifted to a see-now, buy-now model, you can't buy what you see on the runway—because it won't be available for several months, and because often a lot of the clothes never even go into production (bigger brands make most of their money off of shoes and bags). But then, it's not really for consumers at all, anyway. The shows were originally for buyers, and for print magazine editors for whom the season-ahead schedule is relevant to their pace (fall/winter collections show in February; spring/summer shows in September). But as more and more print magazines folded, most coverage of NYFW became less centered around the shows themselves and more about the attendees—and specifically where people sit (the curation of a front row, for example, has the power to make headlines) and what they wear.

And oh, what I wore! Though the street style photography frenzy had probably reached critical mass, the pressure to turn up in the absolute newest clothes and accessories—so new they weren't available to anyone yet—had never felt greater. I learned that there was no amount of preparedness that was out of proportion to the pressure; every fashion season I set up a rack in my living room and spent a week visiting showrooms to borrow samples, because my own clothes would truly never cut it, and if I could have one less thing to worry about, great. Borrowing clothes was a lot of fun if you're a sample size—a size zero, basically, to fit the runway models—which I was for a few years. It was like playing dress up, only with clothes I'd probably never be able to afford, and I had to wear them in front of the most notable fashion people in the world, and then on the subway.

Obviously, this is a great perk for a very, very tiny group of people, which creates an implicit hierarchy: those who can borrow, and those who are left to fend for themselves. And generally it's the borrowed outfits—the clothes no one has seen before—that get photographed by street style photographers, and so the street style stars that popped up in every magazine roundup remained the same size. Some publications made a concerted effort to feature size diversity, and others like *InStyle* at one point pledged to feature *only* plus-size women in their slideshows online. Those were the exceptions, though. From the outside, if you only looked at photographs of Fashion Week, it would appear that only thin white women attended. That was very much not the case.

But back to Fashion Week's slow, stressful descent into irrelevancy. In addition to understanding that consumers want immediacy, we also knew that they want diversity of all kinds: race, size, age, gender. But I think someone forgot to tell the designers that. Or, worse, they knew and simply did not care. Season after season, a parade of skinny young white women filled almost every runway, and everyone took out their phones to document them, unquestioning.

Just how white and thin was it? The year of my first Fashion Week, the *New York Times* reported that 82.7 percent of the models were white. It was also the first year ever that a plus-size designer presented a collection. A few years later, according to a report put out by the Fashion Spot, in February 2018, 62.7 percent of all models on the runway were white. The size-diversity numbers are even more troubling: 1.1 percent of the models were plus-size. The rest of the models were treated like clothes hangers. They looked, in all frankness, like starving, cold teenagers—at best they were very thin; at worst (and more commonly) you could see all their bones, the bags under their glazed-over eyes.

We all became so used to the shape of models' bodies that,

even if we could abstractly acknowledge that that's not what average, healthy women look like, it felt like everyone just pretended it was normal—because what would happen if we actually considered the amount of starvation required to look like that? I'm sure some of the models were naturally thin, but the vast majority were so clearly suffering from severe eating disorders that it's a wonder to me they could even walk down the runway at all.

The continued silence around the issue was particularly ironic once that empowerment turned into an aesthetic. In 2017 multiple shows had models walking in variations on a theme of girl-power T-shirts, selling a political ideology that somehow didn't extend to the actual women modeling the messaging. Not to mention the editors in the audience and their newfound concern with feminist content—every season, another fashion publication joined the chorus of criticism, pointing out the ways fashion is failing women, mourning the lack of diversity on the runways, and often very smartly deconstructing the problematic values of the industry.

And yet: these same writers and editors still went to the shows. As many shows as possible, even. Myself included. We put effort into our appearances; we scheduled our lives around Fashion Week. We posted about it all month long on our social media accounts. And in doing so, we were complicit. Even though I knew better than to blindly worship designers, I couldn't help but get swept up in the shimmery madness of it all; how do you turn down a front-row seat when you've been fighting for years to be taken seriously? You don't. Or at least, *I* didn't.

Take, for example, the global editorial obsession with Chanel, the pinnacle of couture. I don't know a single fashion person who doesn't have a weakness for the brand. It's a name you almost have to whisper. *Chanel.* And yet. Gabrielle Chanel is rumored to have been a Nazi, and her successor, Karl Lagerfeld, was notorious for his very public hatred of—as he put it—fat women and ugly women. Recently deceased, his legacy lingers—he's considered one of the most influential fashion icons of all time, and one of the most beloved. But his definition of beauty was limited to thin white women, and though he indisputably made beautiful work, his personal biases helped uphold the idea that only a certain kind of person with a certain kind of body should have access to luxury fashion. None of that is a secret; it's an inconvenient fact that was largely ignored by otherwise feminist-oriented editors. Even I was once in a branded editorial for Refinery29 featuring women named Gabrielle in celebration of Chanel's Gabrielle bag. I got paid in a gift of the bag featured, which is still the most expensive thing I own and sits on its own shelf in my bedroom.

It was easy to blame the designers for the glorification of eating disorders. It seemed like such an easy fix: cast curve models. Make the clothes to fit them. It felt like laziness, like a willful disregard for not only women's bodies but our well-being. But by continuing to show up in droves for these shows, we were telling them that we were okay with it. We forgave the designer for being a fatphobic misogynist if the clothes were super pretty.

I am fully implicating myself in the problem, but I also felt that if I had stopped going to shows, rather than any sort of wave being made, I'd just quickly be forgotten and everything would continue as is. I had no delusions of grandeur about my own participation and what it signified. Yes, when I was an editor in chief, I tended to get a front-row seat, but there was a line of people behind me who would have loved to have taken it. I could have stopped going on principle, and actually every season I fantasized about doing just that, but at a time in media when layoffs happen faster than anyone could keep track of, I worried about reminding my peers that I was still there. I worried that if I didn't go, the assumption would be that I'd given up. When I left my job, I realized how ridiculous that was. No one was keeping tabs on me like that. And leaving a job isn't seen as giving up, either—when I announced my resignation, my peers completely understood why. Some even expressed jealousy.

For any real change to happen in the fashion industry, all of the editors and bloggers and influencers would have to come together and agree to stop showing up for designers that aren't making an active effort to improve diversity. That would mean going to probably four or five shows as opposed to the nearly one hundred that happen during New York Fashion Week alone.

Those four or five designers per season that are working to

make a difference—usually queer people and people of color—were worth showing up for. Shows like Chromat, Christian Siriano, and Gypsy Sport became known for runways that felt more like celebrations than showcases. It was an emotional experience, going to a show with proper representation. Runway shows usually featured too-loud music and silent crowds, but at these, people cheered. Moments like when Chromat sent every size model down the runway in T-shirts that read "Sample Size" and when well-known plus-size models like Ashley Graham or Paloma Elsesser appeared always elicited claps and shouts. I'd look at my peers around me, and we'd all have tears in our eyes. There was the time the trans actress Laverne Cox opened the show for a brand that was featuring only plus sizes—she burst onto the runway in a dramatic, voluminous red dress, twirling gloriously. We all documented the experience on our social media, eager to get eyeballs on people whose values are worth promoting. But then we gathered up our belongings and ran to the next show.

Fashion isn't solely to blame for the eating disorder epidemic—there are tons of factors that contribute to someone's pathology—but it certainly isn't helping. While there is, in my opinion, no right or wrong way to have a body, according to an often-cited study from 1996, runway models are thinner than 98 percent of American women. If fashion shows are for the 2 percent of women who see themselves reflected on the runways, the rest of America is left to feel not just excluded from something they might otherwise enjoy but like their bodies aren't good enough for it.

And as someone who was struggling with my own eating issues, Fashion Week felt like one giant trigger, and I had to assume it was for other people, too. It was hard for me to look at my peers without wondering if they were currently going hungry to fit into whatever fabulous thing they had on. If someone was particularly rude, my first thought was that she probably hadn't eaten that day. It took mental gymnastics deserving of a gold medal for me to get dressed for it once I couldn't throw on any borrowed sample I wanted, to not spend the month ahead of the event skipping meals and working out obsessively. February, when any extra flesh can be bundled, was easier than September, when it was usually at least eighty degrees outside and there was no hiding. But either way I ended up spending a gross amount of time worrying about my own appearance, undoing the years I spent trying to do the exact opposite. Even if I landed on something that I felt good about, overall it was my worst look: that spiral of anxiety and then shame over the anxiety. Watching models walk down the runway, I had to force myself to not focus on their bodies. All this, postrecovery, just to stay afloat.

In our current political landscape, when there are more men accused of sexual assault on the Supreme Court than there are women of color, this can seem superficial. It's just fashion, after all—surely there are more important things to worry about, like, um, our fundamental rights over our own bodies. But how you clothe that body is a right, too. It's not news that you can be feminist and also love fashion—that's one thing my generation has definitely proven. But by continuing to participate in an event that seems to take women's well-being out of the equation, the message is that feminism only applies when it's convenient. It's a deeply harmful inconsistency, evidence of an ideology that makes exceptions for major institutions because of things like vanity, and advertising dollars, and FOMO.

If there's any hope of making the world a more equal place for women, we have to look at every industry, at every event, at every single moment in our lives and be honest about the power structures we're helping to uphold. Just because Fashion Week is exciting and glamorous and Instagram friendly doesn't mean it should be exempt from this lens. If anything, a predominantly female event should be the ultimate space for equality and empowerment—not just a space with the occasional girl-power T-shirt.

For as long as I can remember, exclusivity has been at the core of fashion. Aspirational for everyone, accessible to almost no one. It's a totally backward, unsustainable concept. At a certain point, people are bound to get sick of longing for something they can never attain, and they'll start to create their own fashion on their own terms. That's already starting to happen and is probably why NYFW is becoming such a disorganized nightmare.

Fashion Week in February 2019 was more disorganized than ever. There were two shows in a row that I couldn't get into because the people at the door had accidentally let in so many influencers who didn't actually have seats that the venues hit capacity. A few PR people for the brands spotted me in the line and tried to get me in, but the security guards wouldn't let them. Rather than waiting outside in the freezing cold for the chance to access my own seat, I said fuck it and I went home to Wallace and the dogs. I had absolutely zero FOMO. I was annoyed that I had to spend so much time waiting for nothing, but really, I was starting to feel like it was totally punk rock for people to start crashing what is typically the most inaccessible event of the year.

My first Fashion Week, when I set the alarm off, I was desperate to find a hidden exit to sneak out of. But the only way out was through: in full view of the editors, the models, the glam teams, the publicists. That was the only way to open the door to real change, too—not quietly, not out the back, but with everyone watching. And a few years later, I was more than happy to take a step back and watch other people pry open those doors, literally and symbolically. After all, I finally had somewhere I'd rather be.

8

Bone Broth

In the early spring of 2017, I was cast as the anchor of an exclusive weekly news show. I had barely begun talking about my anorexia, and the thought of having to be on camera every week made me feel like I'd have to put recovery on hold and stay as skinny as possible, which I had just learned meant the show would be "a trigger." But I also didn't feel like I could say no—it would be, I was told, an amazing opportunity for me to get my voice and face out there to an international audience. I was picking what stories we'd cover and then riffing on everything off the top of my head on camera, as I'd proven incapable of using a teleprompter. It was literally a show centered around my authentic, unfiltered thoughts on pop culture, and people were spending a lot of money to get those thoughts out there. I knew it would be counterproductive for my mental health, but it felt worth it.

Throughout the filming of the show, I made it a point to explicitly prioritize stories of body positivity and to promote racial diversity within every vertical. It ran the gamut from serious—talking about racism as Trump-inspired white supremacy rallies took place across the country—to playful, highlighting a fashion brand that had an entirely vagina-themed collection during NYFW. This was feminism for 2017: fast-paced, content oriented, based on progressive values, and hosted by me, a clinically underweight white twentysomething.

On the first day of filming, we stopped to order lunch. The producer asked the team what we all wanted. Someone said, "I'd love a bone broth." I hadn't heard of bone broth; it had yet to become fully trendy and was still kind of a fringe diet thing. Everyone else had, though, and I was quickly filled in on all of its benefits and variations. Protein without the calories! So many nutrients! You can add turmeric! It's basically like a meal! As everyone chatted excitedly about bone broth, something took hold in my brain: Bone broth, yes. That's what I wanted. What I needed! Bone broth was the compromise between starving myself and committing to recovery. I was still looking for loopholes in the plan I'd agreed to with my doctor, and this seemed like a good one. We all ordered it for lunch, and after I drank it, someone remarked to me that my eyes looked more alive.

Bone broth, I would like to clarify, is *not* a replacement for a meal. But because it's temporarily so filling, for many who find themselves searching for the latest greatest solution to the problem of needing to eat but wanting to look starving, it was seen as just that. It joined a long line of alleged meal substitutes— green juice, smoothies, protein bars—and diet trends: keto, Whole30, Paleo, cleansing, fasting.

An obsession with healthy eating is called orthorexia. It's not a diagnosis in the *DSM*, but it was defined in the mid-1990s to describe what one doctor noticed in some patients: an overt fixation with eating healthy, or eating "right." Wanting to eat healthy is not a mental illness, but restructuring your life so that you *only* eat foods you define as healthy can be. I didn't really develop orthorexia; I chose to just not eat anything. But orthorexia was all around me and in many ways enabled me. Among certain people there's just an assumption that if you are skinny you also have your own custom list of foods to avoid. Some people have told me that their list comes from a doctor; others have said an allergist; others still tell me they base it on a DNA test that tells them the foods that make them puffy. They often plan their lives around these lists—they can only go to certain restaurants, or they won't go to restaurants at all. Their self-imposed dietary restrictions dictate every aspect of their lives.

Interestingly enough, what I haven't heard is anyone call this behavior dieting. Dieting, in our performatively woke world, is not cool. Orthorexia, instead, is flaunted as more of a lifestyle, one that is structured around an idea of healthiness. It is very Instagram friendly, making it impossible to escape. And when you're trying to get over something like anorexia and are surrounded by people who "don't have an eating disorder" but are "trying intermittent fasting" or are "taking a break from sugar and dairy and carbs and alcohol and fat" or maybe are "doing an olive oil cleanse for my liver," which involves not eating anything but a shot glass worth of olive oil once a day for a week (yes), the line between healthy and not healthy becomes very, very blurry.

It's hard not to feel anger toward people who exhibit this behavior, since it usually comes with an air of moral superiority. Orthorexics tend to be convinced that there are "right" foods and "wrong" foods. The concept of "right food" and a "best way to eat" isn't just oppressive for those who think that way; it's alienating for the people around them, which causes even more damage: left to their own devices, they can implement whatever obsessive diet structure they want without a witness.

My nutritionist, it seemed, was used to people who have orthorexia. In one of our first sessions together, she wanted to make a list of foods that inspired fear, categorizing food into stuff I would eat and stuff I absolutely wouldn't. She didn't quite get that I was willing to eat a bite of anything; it was quantity that was the problem. Or maybe it wasn't: we had a full page of foods that I wouldn't mind eating, until she said, "Banana bread."

"It's not that I'm afraid of it," I said slowly. "I just don't see a point."

"What do you mean?" she asked, sounding genuinely confused. "Banana bread can be a great snack."

"But, like, what even is it?" I said. "Is it dessert? Is it bread? There's no point. It's dessert. I wouldn't eat dessert as a snack. I wouldn't eat a piece of bread, either."

She said, "Plenty of people do."

I was stunned. "But why?"

She was curious about why banana bread as a snack was so mind-blowing to me, so she pushed me to elaborate. "What is banana bread bringing up for you right now?"

"Nothing!" I insisted. And then the memories came flooding back and I said, "Oh. Well . . ."

Julia, my fraternal twin, who has always been smaller than me, couldn't put on weight when we were kids. I could. So I'd drink skim milk, and she drank whole milk; my mom bought her a whole pile of junk food at the grocery store every week, and she'd devour all of it, seeming to digest it as quickly as it went into her mouth. Her favorite thing was Entenmann's banana cake. You know the one: a big square cake with yellow frosting and dark-brown frosting accents. Julia used to eat it with a fork out of the box. Sometimes she'd eat more than half of it in one sitting; sometimes that would be her dinner. I understood that the cake was for her and not for me. Banana bread and banana cake have become synonymous in my memory; it's something that I shouldn't have.

All of this came, surprisingly, tumbling out of my mouth. My nutritionist asked if I'd talked to my therapist about it. I laughed. I hadn't even thought of it until that moment. And really, it didn't seem like an important memory compared to everything else I was talking about in therapy. The next week my nutritionist brought two slices of banana bread to my session, and we ate it together, which she seemed to think was a big milestone, and I frankly found it kind of annoying.

She was also trying to convince me to work out less, an idea that made me bristle. But I was somewhat self-aware about the intensity of my workouts; I knew it was too much. I no longer was sore from my go-to barre class, but not going made me feel awful. I was planning my life around it, often lying to people about where I was. I'd cancel plans with friends to go. If I couldn't get into an evening class, I'd go in the middle of the workday. I kept yoga pants in my purse. I even ran to a class in the middle of helping my sister move, a decision so selfish I am literally cringing as I type it.

I had started taking barre classes the previous year for a story. I'd launched a series called Bootcamp; the idea was that since the majority of my team were self-proclaimed couch potatoes, it would be funny and engaging to send people to different cult workout classes and review them. I picked barre because it sounded about as far outside of my comfort zone as I could go—I hadn't done anything resembling ballet since I was a toddler. I don't like dancing, and no one would ever call me graceful. So a free three months of standing on my toes sounded like it would be, at the very least, a hilarious story.

I had also just gained a bunch of weight—happy weight, from my new relationship with the Scorpio, though I was far from happy about it. The instructor, after the first class, offered to take "before" pictures of me from all angles, which I saved in my phone in a folder I titled "Body." She said, "You're small, so you're going to see results very quickly." I figured she was just being nice. I didn't feel small. I felt huge. I hated the photos of me in my yoga pants and sports bra. I didn't recognize the rolls in my lower back or the curve of my stomach when I stood to the side.

Barre was really hard at first. I could barely keep up with the moves, not to mention actually do them. I felt awkward and embarrassed. It didn't help that the class I was going to was full of famous models, actresses, and other editors; I was told that many women love barre because it elongates your muscles, meaning it makes you lean rather than bulky. It's a favorite among fashion-industry types who are chasing that long-and-lean body thing. I woke up sore every single day, in parts of my body I didn't know existed. But a couple of months in, something magical happened: I could do it, and I loved it. I started to see muscles forming. I felt strong. I wrote a gushy review of my journey, and the manager of the studio thanked me with a year membership for free.

Having free classes made me feel obligated to go as much as possible, lest I let such a generous offer go to waste. So I did. At first, four times a week, then five, then every day. Then I noticed some of the models were taking two classes in a row. "They're trying to lose weight before Fashion Week," an editor whispered to me. I rolled my eyes, agreeing it was ridiculous. Then I waited for her to leave so I could double book myself for classes that weekend.

It's hard to work out when you're starving, at first, and then it's not: my doctor explained to me that starvation makes you run on adrenaline. Though every class got harder and harder to begin, by the halfway point I'd feel like I was floating. By the end of class I'd feel so sad that I had to try not to cry. I was surprised to find myself with a workout addiction. And it was funny, really, to have gotten addicted to that specific workout class, which prided itself on being body positive and absolutely never used language of weight loss but instead encouraged people to just do what feels good. There was nothing in the structure of the method to make me feel bad about myself. That time, it all came from me and what I walked in the door carrying.

At this point, I also had a weird fixation with smoothies. For whatever reason, I was able to justify drinking a meal more than chewing it. There was a Juice Press a few blocks from my office, and I'd go every day for lunch, which was as much a horrendous waste of money as it was a poor excuse for a meal. But a lot of my coworkers did it, too, and it became very normalized. I remember one editor who would have a spicy juice shot for lunch and drink the whole thing while she paid. Others added probiotics to otherwise fiber-filled drinks in order to constantly "cleanse," aka give themselves diarrhea. When I told my nutritionist about my Juice Press habit, she pulled up the menu and pointed out which smoothie I should be having that was an actual substitute for lunch, and I agreed to switch to it instead of the lighter one I'd been slurping. The next time one of my work friends went on a smoothie run, she asked if I wanted the usual, and I told her I needed something with a little more calories. In a teasing voice, she said, "What, did you lose *too* much weight?" as though that weren't possible.

One day in barre, midsquat, I looked around and realized that I was the smallest person in the room. It was shocking to see. I looked . . . puny. The next time I saw my doctor I told her about it and she said, "That awareness is your brain flickering back on." She was proud of me.

As I tried to cut down on barre classes, I thought I'd check out another kind of workout to see if diversifying my routine would make me feel better about doing less. I went to a HIIT class, which stands for high-intensity interval training. It was coed, which I wasn't used to; usually there are just one or two guys in barre. The instructor came over to teach me one of the positions and I said, "Oh, I know this one from barre; I stick my bootie out, right?" She quickly shushed me, saying, "We don't use that word here. The men don't like it." I was totally taken aback. Since when had I ever not used a word because men don't like it? She continued, "It's too feminine." That just about blew my mind. I didn't go back—not because I didn't like the workout (I loved it) but because I couldn't imagine having to tailor my vocabulary to avoid accidentally emasculating someone.

Speaking of gender, I've never worked in an office that's not majority-female, so I don't know if this phenomenon happens in more gender-balanced spaces, but once I started focusing on my recovery, I was astounded by how my office had become a bubble of disordered eating. At one point I noticed that a particular coworker had dropped a ton of weight really quickly, and so I asked her privately if she was okay; she replied that she was doing Whole30 (a strict elimination diet), as was her entire row of desks. They had all decided to do it together. She was amused at my alarm.

This is not uncommon. A former deputy editor at a women's magazine told me about a boss who would walk around the office talking at full volume nearly every day "about Whole30, or 'being naughty,' or whatever diet she was on to lose weight for whatever thing. She also commented on everyone else's food and would loudly compliment thin women on being 'so damn skinny.'" After ten years of being on top of her own eating disorder, she told me, it was this environment that caused her to relapse. Another editor who worked at what she described to me as a "woke female fashion publication" recalled once preparing a bagel for herself in the office kitchen only to have a coworker come in and say, "*Carbs*. You are so brave." She continued, "They were not kidding, and I remember feeling distinctly like a garbage monster." This same person told me that at the time, she was very thin, not so much because of body dysmorphia but "more about stress, lack of affordable and nutritional food options, and working myself to the bone." She went on to describe something I am too familiar with: the lack of lunchtime at fashion publications. "Most people worked through it, didn't eat at all, or ate, like, cucumbers." All this, again, at companies creating empowerment-driven content, many of which were simultaneously implementing size-diversity missions.

Another former fashion editor at a magazine preaching women's empowerment told me that the editor in chief said to her, "Let's not wear that dress ever again. We look pregnant." She was there from 2013 to 2017, when digital feminism was really taking off. Meanwhile, she told me, her eating disorder affected her work; she gained thirty to forty pounds and "constantly felt like I wasn't good enough. That I didn't look the part. [I] wanted to hide my body." While she dealt with the comments her boss made about her appearance and other institutionalized pressures to look a certain way, she observed other people—people who fit the mold—climbing the ranks. Her eating disorder became a defense: "I took it all out on myself by using it as a way to cope with really negative, toxic feelings."

Women like me aren't supposed to talk about things like this, about the ways that all-female spaces aren't automatically the feminist utopias we want them to be. But eating disorders have the highest mortality rate of any mental illness, and I can't remain silent about something that is actually killing people and yet is culturally—and, it seems, professionally—glorified. One woman who used to work for a major fashion house recently told me that her coworkers would regularly faint from hunger in the office, which everyone else would then gossip and joke about. She said she had hoped that working in a space that was mostly women and gay men would have liberated them from those kinds of pressures. Instead, as I understand, it was more like a petri dish.

At work, as in life, women are under incredible pressure to be our best selves. We have shattered the glass ceiling and now we must burst through the space where it once was, sparkling and glowing phoenixes, deserving of wealth and recognition and equality. We must battle the imposter syndrome that we are told we all suffer from. We must get promoted, and if we don't, we must find new, more impressive work. We must document it on Instagram. And because we have been told, again and again and again, in infomercials and talk shows and magazines and movies, that inside every woman there's a thinner, better woman waiting to be released, even the most levelheaded of us fail to separate the shape of our bodies from the merit of our work.

And what's even more disturbing is the way that behavior is rewarded. An editor confirmed to me that at two different large media companies, she observed that people who conformed to the "ideal standard" were valued more than others; "their relationships with management were positive and more outward facing." The aforementioned deputy editor told me, "When I worked at one magazine there was another editor that was thinner, younger—she would go on TV to talk about my stories." A high-level creative at a women's media company had a similar experience: "As a plus woman I was constantly left out of front and center forward-facing PR. Only the 'coolest'-looking people were paraded in front of press."

And a former Condé Nast and Hearst editor recalled that from 2005 to 2016, she'd get advice to "dress for the job you want, not the job you have," but: "That wasn't easy for someone who was obese," because, obviously, fashion has a long way to go in terms of plus-size options. The year she was laid off, she says she lost one hundred pounds, "and definitely felt I had more opportunities afterward as a result of the weight loss."

While none of the women I spoke to for this chapter thought that this was unique to the industry in question, many of them pointed out that it's just more of an open secret in women's media. The deputy editor said, "It's weirdly hidden in women's media because everyone is nominally feminist and body positive—so it's even more insidious." She continued, "Bonding over barre and Paleo is almost the female equivalent of men going golfing. It excludes people."

The toxicity of openly complaining about your body or bragging about your diet at work cannot be understated. Many people told me about how damaging it was to have to constantly overhear people talk about how much they hate their bodies, and the creative mentioned above said that fashion teams in particular would talk openly about starving in preparation for New York Fashion Week. As one freelance writer expressed, "When people complain about something they don't like about themselves and it's something I also have but never really paid attention to or felt bad about, suddenly I wonder if I should feel bad about it. Then I fixate on it and berate myself for not noticing and worry about how people saw me." I personally never would have started my bone broth and smoothie habits if the people around me hadn't been flaunting their liquid lunches, and I'll never forget the one time I brought a croissant for breakfast and an editor said to me, "I don't know how you justify eating that shit," or the time I got ice cream for my team only to have a marketing person walk by us and say, "Wow, I can't remember the last time I ate that." In those moments I was annoyed, but from the other side, I just feel deeply concerned for them.

Once I was running my own office, I had very few employees who did this. Most of the ones I worried the most about were either laid off in the print closing or left shortly thereafter. There were only a couple of people remaining who said things like, "I'm not going to eat until Fashion Week," and I just had to roll my eyes at them, throwing an invisible wall up to not get sucked in.

As for that news show I decided to starve for? Well . . . as it turned out, even though we had sold an up-to-the-minute pop culture news series, the platform required a three-day approval process before anything could be uploaded. That meant by the time the episodes went live, the news was stale, so we couldn't really promote it on our social platforms—calling it news would make us look out of touch. So in the end barely anyone watched it, except my friends and family, really. My team decided to reframe it as a proof of concept that we could take to other buyers in the hopes of a more lucrative partnership. But when the ten-episode run wrapped, leadership had changed, and interest faded. It had been, in the end, a massive waste of money and time, which was actually a really good lesson for me: I had been so worried about my weight for truly no reason. Not that there's any real reason to do what I did, though.

At a party in the middle of a recent NYFW, I ran into an acquaintance who is an editor at another magazine. In coded words, we both admitted to feeling totally traumatized by having to watch skinny models walk runways all day, every day. She said, "I was just starting to feel okay with having flesh," and we both laughed, a little bit sadly. I thought it was such a beautiful way to put it, because, really, when you try to lose weight, that's what you're battling: your own flesh.

When I got home, I headed right for my bed. I was tired from the evening of fabulous events, but more than that, I was exhausted on an existential level from a lifetime of trying to survive in a world that seemed hell-bent on keeping women small, figuratively and literally. I felt like I'd been paying a toll to be successful, and that toll was taken from my body, draining me under the pretense of making me more powerful. And I was ready to take my power back.

9

Entitled Millennial

As a kid I didn't really have celebrity crushes, until Bright Eyes. Conor Oberst in 2003–2007 embodied a kind of tortured androgyny that I found myself unreasonably drawn to. Formally a pretty levelheaded high schooler, I was suddenly ripping out pages of magazines, entranced by the way his T-shirt clung to his hip bones, dreaming of my hands in his asymmetrical hair. I don't think I ever actually fantasized about having sex with him; it was a very innocent daydream that mostly involved kissing and spooning and sharing clothes. I learned how to play early Bright Eyes songs on the guitar, the ones from the late '90s when he's barely a teenager recording songs about girls in his bedroom on an 8-track. I bought an 8-track. Later Bright Eyes albums became more lush with instruments, more generous with harmonies, overall more sophisticated, and I imagined myself evolving alongside him. I trusted completely that if only we could meet, he'd feel the same way.

In 2005 he released two albums at once: *I'm Wide Awake, It's Morning*, which was catchy and folksy and romantic and heartbreaking, and *Digital Ash in a Digital Urn*, which was dark and dancy and sexy. I was a sophomore in high school, and my life was positively transformed by these two records; in an overwrought, melodramatic way I felt seen by their duality, by the way they sounded so different but both contained pain and secrecy, truth and longing. I got his haircut, long bangs in the front and cropped short in the back. My best friend and I got tickets to see him play at Webster Hall, an eighteen-plus show, and somehow snuck in. He played *Digital Ash* all the way through, backlit so that he was just a thin glowing outline, even though we were in front leaning against the stage. The next show I went to was at a venue called City Hall, way more civilized with stadium seating, and he played songs from *I'm Wide Awake* while wearing a cowboy hat, all the lights on.

"You're looking skinny like a model with your eyes all painted black," he sang in a slightly off-key whisper, not to me but also not *not* to me.

Years went by. The summer between my freshman and sophomore years of college, when I started sleeping with my roommate and my whole world was turning upside down and inside out, a friend claimed to have met Conor Oberst at a bar. We sat around the dorm kitchen smoking pot out of a hookah as she regaled us with the story. Apparently there was a dive on St. Mark's Place right near Tompkins Square Park that he was known to frequent, though how everyone knew that except me was unclear. At any rate, she'd gone with the hope of catching a glimpse of him. She said Oberst had not only been there but bought her a drink, and then another, and then another, and then when she'd tried to leave, he became pushy and aggressive, she remembered. "He was a total asshole!" she said. By then my fandom had simmered, but it was still disappointing to hear that the shy, almost feminine man whose shaky voice had been the soundtrack to my adolescence was nothing but another jerk.

Years later still, a commenter on xoJane, Joanie Faircloth of North Carolina, would accuse him of raping her when she was sixteen. Conor Oberst, who had sung anti-Bush songs in the early 2000s on late-night cable TV and in general been a beacon of male redeemability for emo-feminist teen girls everywhere, was suddenly tainted with controversy.

He ended up suing Joanie for libel, which was very obviously totally outrageous and offensive: he was trying to silence her. I wrote about it and was contacted directly by his publicist, who said that in the trial everything would be cleared up. There was never a trial, though. Joanie issued a public apology retracting her accusation, and Conor released a statement accepting it. The story was used in the media as an example of how one person's internet comments can affect someone's entire reputation—a cautionary tale about false accusations.

In hindsight, his angst, which he was known for, was always out of proportion to his privilege, but I had trusted it blindly. And there were other indie musicians I'd felt similarly about; when I was a senior in high school, at an indie rock show at the now-defunct Sound Fix Records in Williamsburg, the lead singer grabbed me from the front row and pulled me onstage, holding me tightly in his sweaty arms while he sang "Memories" by Leonard Cohen into my face:

> I walked up to the tallest and the blondest girl
> I said, look, you don't know me now, but very soon you will
> So won't you let me see
> I said won't you let me see
> I said won't you let me see
> Your naked body?

After the last word, he cast me back into the crowd. Hearing the story the next day, my parents were horrified. It took me nearly a decade to empathize with their reaction. It was a thrilling moment, but I also know an adult man probably wouldn't get away with doing that to a teenager today. There are certain male figures we were just told to believe in, to trust. Our rock gods. Our politicians. Our medical professionals. A cornerstone of reaching adult womanhood is realizing that this is a myth—that men, no matter what their profession or how deeply their work speaks to you, can be dangerous.

As feminists, we fight to make the world safer for ourselves and each other. We're taught to reclaim our time, to take what has been stolen from us. A big part of that is physical: our bodily safety, our access to spaces, the space we take up. It's all connected. Thinking about the role the patriarchy plays in eating disorders, then, is a total mindfuck. Here we are, successful, smart women, feminists, perfectionists, usually, trying to be as small as possible.

But is it smallness we're chasing, or is it something else entirely? In *Eating in the Light of the Moon*, Dr. Anita Johnson references a societal imbalance of the masculine and feminine as the root of female disordered eating. Taught to value the masculine traits of linear productivity, rationality, and financial success, modern Western culture shuns traits of the divine feminine: emotion, intuition, relationships. Keenly aware of this loss but unable to pinpoint exactly what it's a loss of, there's a certain kind of woman who mistakes the emotional hunger for a literal one. She fills this void, then, with an obsessive fixation on food and, subsequently, tries to control the shape of her body, the dips and curves that mark it biologically female in a world that prioritizes masculinity.

This is so common that an obsession with weight loss is considered a pretty standard part of being a woman. Most of us don't call it an eating disorder. And maybe it's not always one. There's a notable difference between disordered eating and an eating disorder. But still: We say we're too busy to have lunch, or too tired to eat breakfast. Or we're just really into wellness right now and are trying Whole30, or are doing a juice cleanse, or a raw vegan diet. We're flushing out the toxins, we're cutting out dairy and carbs and alcohol; we heard something about nightshade vegetables and inflammation so we no longer eat anything red. We tie it to events: Fashion Week, wedding season, summer. The end result is the same: we take up less and less physical space. Sometimes it feels like the aesthetic goal is to be as tiny as possible without disappearing entirely—otherwise known as dying.

A friend with a similar diagnostic history once said to me that at her worst, she knew her anorexia could kill her, but she didn't care so long as she died skinny. When you're diagnosed with an eating disorder, you learn a lot about what it would take to kill you. Eating below seven hundred calories per day, for example, is when your body starts to shut down. Even if you don't literally starve to death, you're setting yourself up for fatal disease down the line. Like a heart attack.

Hence, after the blood test results from my first visit came back, my doctor wrote me a prescription to get an EKG. She said that because of how much weight I'd lost, she had to make sure I didn't have heart disease. I went alone in the middle of the workday. I always went to these appointments alone, embarrassed and not wanting to burden anyone with the situation that I felt I had created.

I went to an urgent care clinic that just happened to have

an EKG machine. I didn't make an appointment. A young man took me in the back and sat at a computer while asking me routine intake questions about my medical history. It had been a very long time since I'd seen a male medical professional of any kind; all of my doctors were women. But I tried to trust it. It was 2017. It would be fine.

But it wasn't: After asking me if I was sexually active (I was), he gave me a weird lingering look and asked me if I had a boyfriend or a husband. He continued to stare when I clarified that I was gay, and then he told me to take all my clothes off for the test. He left while I did so, and then came back. I'd hastily tried to tie the gown over my chest, which made him laugh, a condescending scoff. He untied it and started attaching sensors to my bare torso.

I'd learn later that you don't have to be naked to get an EKG. Patients can keep their gowns on; in fact, they usually do, with whoever is administering the test moving the gown around in order to fix the sensors on.

He told me to lie still. Placing the sensors around my bare chest, he loomed over me and asked, "So, do you ever date guys?"

I said, "Why is that relevant?"

He said, sounding annoyed, "It's not. I'm just curious." And then he said, "How long have you been with your girlfriend?"

I said, "A few months, but I'm still not sure why that is relevant to this."

He reminded me to lie still. While he ran the EKG machine, a hot tear slid sideways out of my left eye. I was mortified but didn't really have the words for why. I said nothing when he finished, waited until he was fully out of the room before shakily getting up and getting dressed. A woman came in with the results, and before she could tell me that everything looked fine, I blurted out what had just happened, beginning to cry. Her eyes grew wide, but the rest of her face remained neutral, hard to read. "I'm sorry that happened," she said, and promised to tell her supervisor. Embarrassed and unsure what else to do, I fled, just about diving into a cab.

A few minutes later my phone rang. It was the manager of the clinic calling to tell me it had all been a misunderstanding: the man operating the EKG had only meant to finish getting my medical history, she said. He was supposed to do it at the computer but to save time had completed the questions during the test. "Are you trying to tell me that on your intake form, it says, 'Do you ever date guys?'" I shouted into the phone. She repeated, patronizingly, that it was all a misunderstanding. She told me she had daughters, and she understood why I could have misinterpreted his intentions. I said, "It was sexual harassment, and I think you know that." She said she would call me back.

My EKG results had been normal, but my experience wasn't: in addition to his manipulating me into being unnecessarily naked, the line of questioning was, clearly, not procedure.

He kept his job, though. Meanwhile the clinic promised to implement sensitivity training for all employees, to make sure it wouldn't happen again. I had been a sacrificial lamb.

This was April 2017. Just six months later, in October, Harvey Weinstein would be accused of sexual misconduct by nearly eighty women, and #MeToo would begin trending on Twitter, turning into a movement. In January 2018, Larry Nassar would be sentenced to 175 years in prison for decades of sexual misconduct while working as the doctor for the USA Gymnastics team. And in October 2018, in glaring defiance to the progress of the #MeToo movement, Brett Kavanaugh would become the second man accused of sexual misconduct to join the Supreme Court. It's hard to imagine what the repercussions would have been for my EKG tech if he'd stripped me naked and interrogated me about my sexuality on an exam table just a few months later. I'd like to think it would be more than mandatory sensitivity training, but who knows?

Like most people, I have dozens of stories about times men, and a few women, have treated me in a way that can be categorized as sexual misconduct. This was far from the worst one. But it was the first time someone who was actually supposed to be helping me did it. I had sought the help of a stranger and been met with predatory behavior, and then, when he was called out for it, he somehow persuaded his supervisor to try to gaslight me. I was already well versed in the language of abuse, so I was able to identify it immediately and hold my ground. I wondered about the young woman who Conor Oberst sued for libel. I felt like I couldn't trust anyone with my body. Certainly not the men who worked at this healthcare clinic in Midtown. Not even, really, the doctor who had sent me there in the first place, even though I liked and respected her.

As a teenager, not all my role models were indie dudes. Alongside my Conor Oberst shrine was a picture of Karen O, the lead singer of the Yeah Yeah Yeahs, triumphantly spitting beer from the stage over a mosh pit. I pored over *Bitch* by Elizabeth Wurtzel, underlining and dog-earing. I listened to Sleater-Kinney and Bikini Kill on repeat. I loved Camera Obscura and Feist and Azure Ray and the way their voices sounded mysterious and soft and powerful all at the same time (and, yes, the culture I had access to in the early 2000s was very white). I read Feministing.com, a blog started in 2004 that is largely credited with making feminism cool on the internet. My guitar case had a sticker that said "A woman without a man is like a fish without a bicycle." I had a T-shirt that said "Keep your laws off my body," with a drawing of handcuffs, which got me sent to the principal's office.

Abstractly, being a strong feminist to me meant being in control of my body. But it wasn't until I was an adult that I fully understood what that meant. When I lost weight, I wasn't in control of my body—not really. It was a false sense of ownership. I was still following a rule created for me by patriarchy: be as small as possible. In order to protect myself and restore my agency, I needed to liberate myself from the definition of worth that had loomed over my entire life.

One morning in the spring of 2018, about a year later, I was bringing Kimberly back to Avery on the subway, because yes, we still do that. It was around noon in the middle of the week, and I was on a semicrowded downtown R, Kimberly in her carrier on my lap, which was unzipped so that she could rest her little paws and face on my arm. The train stopped between stations, and the doors between cars opened; a young white man in dirty, ripped clothes burst through them and began pacing up and down the car, asking people for money. When no one gave him any, he pointed to a cut on his forehead from which he was bleeding quite profusely and began screaming a story filled with racial slurs about a man who had allegedly hit him.

He stopped in front of me and said, "I could ruin your day so easily, and you wouldn't even care what happened to me." I wordlessly pulled Kimberly closer to me, staring straight ahead, beyond him. He said, "You're so fucking entitled." And then he said, "Your dog has a better life than I do." I pretended to not hear him. He moved on to the other end of the car, harassing other people. When the train stopped at the next station, he ran by me, wiping blood from his forehead onto Kimberly, who was fast asleep in my arms.

It was my stop, too. No one would make eye contact with me. As I exited the train, I noticed there was a man talking to the train conductor through the window. He had been on a different car but had witnessed a similar incident with the same man. I walked up to them and presented my bloody poodle. I said, "He wiped his blood all over my dog." The train conductor said, "What would you like me to do?" And then started the engine and left. Out of the corner of my eye I suddenly noticed that the man in question was sitting on the benches, hood pulled up, watching me.

I hurried to the top of the steps, desperate to be above ground. When I got to the top, I heard footsteps behind me, and there he was, in my face, shouting, grabbing my arms. I had my phone in my hands and he jumped on me, saying, "I'm going to take your fucking phone," trying to pry my fingers open (mind you, I was also holding Kimberly). I started screaming at the top of my lungs. A woman came running over, shouting too. He scratched my chest, ripping my shirt open, and ran away.

I had to clamp a hand over my mouth to stop screaming. The woman, who I suddenly realized was very young, said, "Sweetie, who was that? Was that your boyfriend?"

I said, "I have no idea who that was," and started to sob. I was shaking violently. I think she hugged me, but I'm not sure. She said, "Hold on," and then she made a phone call, telling the person on the phone she was going to be late for her job interview because she just saw a woman get attacked. I said, "Oh my god, no, please go to your job interview." She told me she was a nurse. She had long acrylic nails and a comforting Long Island accent. I loved her. I insisted she leave, that I was fine. She walked me to the nearest bodega, where with trembling hands I called 911, and then I texted Avery that she had to come meet me.

Avery met me on the corner, and I cried on her shoulder. She gingerly took Kimberly out of my arms (Kimberly was fine—she slept through most of this). I called Wallace, who was uptown. My chest where he scratched me was bright red and splotchy, and hot to the touch. It took the cops nearly half an hour to come, by which point the guy was long gone. They filed a report for harassment, not assault, because my skin didn't break. They told me that in New York City you can go as far as punching someone in the face, and if the skin doesn't break, it's not assault, which was news to me.

Avery waited with me in a coffee shop until Wallace came. Trying to distract me, she told me that recently some guy on the train platform called her a fag and then pushed an open container of chicken lo mein into her face, a double blow since she's vegan. I was supposed to be proud of her for walking away and not getting into a fight, an evolved reaction from how she was in her twenties, but all I could feel was despair. As a butch woman, she's experienced more, and worse, homophobic violence than I ever have. I felt the need to apologize to her for crumbling in the aftermath of an attack that was maybe equally as traumatic as the lo mein story she casually told me, but I couldn't get the words out. I couldn't get any words out at all, and she quickly changed the subject. She left when Wallace got there, and they exchanged worried eye contact. Wallace put her arms around me, and I buried my face in her neck. I felt disconnected from my body. I took a cab home, calling out of work for the rest of the day.

I couldn't stop thinking about how intimate the violence felt—how he'd picked me out of a crowd as someone worth harassing, how he'd put his hands on me, how he'd looked directly into my eyes while he tried to wrench my phone out of my hands. It felt deeply personal, even though he had been a perfect stranger. The police, two white men, had asked, "Do you have any idea why he approached *you*?" I said, "Maybe because I'm a woman?," which made them laugh. I wasn't trying to be funny. But in truth I wasn't the only woman on the train so it wasn't the answer. The question was repeated by other people to whom I recounted the details: *Why you?* I hadn't wondered it until it was posed. For some reason the moment he'd entered the car, I'd felt an inevitability; his rage, as soon as he revealed it, seemed destined to land on me. But I didn't have an explanation. His class-based argument, that Kimberly had a better life than him, was a bizarre comparison and likely untrue; my dog, after all, spent the first half of her life in a wire cage outside, churning out puppies and never learning to walk properly. But even as an animal lover I don't think you can compare human poverty to animal cruelty; it's a false equivalence, and it felt like just an excuse to go after me.

In the year that had passed since the incident with the EKG tech, plenty of other scary things had happened; in addition to the usual daily onslaught of catcalls, one day I ignored a man who said, "Nice legs," as I walked by him—he then proceeded to chase me down the subway platform, screaming in my face about what a "racist slut" I was. He said I was an entitled bitch, and ungrateful, and should learn how to take a compliment, and that I wasn't all that anyway. He was eating a bagel and spitting pieces of it in my face as he ranted. I began shouting, "You need to back the fuck up," which only made him get closer and closer to me, until finally a very tall man came and silently stood between us, making the other guy skulk off.

Following the incident at the doctor's office, my therapist had tried to introduce a theory that I hadn't been ready to hear: that I had, in some way, caused the EKG tech to treat me the way he did. When she suggested this, I was confused and hurt, and I accused her of victim blaming. She quickly apologized and said that's not what she had meant. I couldn't conceive of any other implication. She waited to bring it up again, and when she did, she connected these incidents in a way I could finally hear—she wasn't, she clarified, implying that I did anything inherently wrong. But, after all, they were so similar that I had no choice but to try to analyze my own role, aside from simply being a woman in public. That question came back. *Why me?*

What we landed on as the common thread here and throughout my life was my staunch refusal to be objectified (her words). For better or worse, when men tried to intimidate me, I held my head higher. When they tried to stare me down, I didn't blink. When they screamed at me, I screamed back. When they sexualized me, I acted like they were so worthless they didn't even exist. This, in turn, enraged them. As my therapist pointed out, it's like a mutual triggering; there's a certain kind of man who was set off by my refusal to be objectified, and reacted with rage, which in turn triggered my own rage. It caused situations to escalate very quickly. I am lucky that nothing worse has ever happened to me based on the way I've told aggressive strangers to go fuck themselves rather than trying to neutralize the situation.

I'm not sure why or how or precisely when I became like this. Maybe it was the pediatrician who leaned his crotch into my knees while he looked in my ears so that I could feel, with unforgettable clarity, the exact shape of what lay behind his zipper. Maybe it was the last boy I ever slept with, when I was eighteen, who plied me with beer and then climbed on top of me, whose terrible smelly beard rubbed my face so raw that when he stood up he said, "Wow, you look awful." Or maybe it was the group of drunk men who surrounded me and a friend one night in college at a bodega and began caressing our arms, saying, "How much?" and laughing hysterically. Or the boy in middle school who, while we did homework in his living room, kept taking his dick out to jerk off, staring at me with a mix of rage and hunger, his mother in the next room. Or maybe it was the kid in high school who pretended to be my friend but told everyone I was a slut because I'd kissed one of his friends in my bedroom but then refused to be his girlfriend. Maybe it was the gay guy in college who wouldn't stop grabbing my nipples or the one at a *Nylon* party who grabbed my ass with both his hands and then, as I yelled at him, did it again, laughing. Maybe it was the hundreds of catcalls therein. Or maybe it was the totality of these moments, piling onto my body like mud and then hardening into cement, like armor.

But it's armor I've had for as long as I can remember, a chicken-or-the-egg situation where the chicken is the way certain people have treated me and the egg is my boundaries. I had a crush on a boy in middle school but every time we interacted he would get physical, poking and prodding me, so I would start screaming. Eventually he gave up and started "going out" with one of my friends. One night over AIM I asked him why her and not me, and he said, "Because she flirts back and you just get mad." Flirting? Was that *flirting*? Later, in high school, a boy was teasing me so I cursed him out and he said, "For a quiet girl you sure are a bitch." Was *that* flirting? Why did flirting always feel so . . . invasive?

I was told again and again that something or someone was harmless. A harmless boy. A harmless old man. Harmless flirting. But who gets to decide what counts as harm? Certainly not me, I learned. I quickly got a reputation as someone who couldn't take a joke, which stayed with me through adulthood. When my sisters and I were out at a bar in our early twenties, a bartender squirted me with a water gun, drenching my shirt, and one of my sisters and I got into an argument because it made me want to leave without paying and she said that would be stealing. I didn't care if it was stealing. I just needed to get out of there.

Would it surprise you to learn, at this point, that I have also struggled for my entire life with being painfully shy? I blush when I'm nervous. I'm terrible in group settings—sometimes it's like I forget to talk because I become so focused on observing other people. So this *thing* that happened to me in the presence of aggressive men—this transformation from shy to furious—surprised other people as much as it did me. When you're a shy little girl, you're adorable. When you're a shy adult woman, you're a bitch. Women I dated used to be confused and frustrated by how forthcoming and warm I'd be one-on-one only to freeze up around their friends. Very few people understood that it was shyness, not coldness.

After what happened with the guy on the subway, I couldn't sleep for weeks. I'd be starting to drift off and then I'd imagine a worst-case scenario. He could have pushed me down the stairs or onto the subway tracks. His scratch could have actually ripped open my skin, not just my shirt. I could have dropped Kimberly in the midst of the scuffle and she could have run into traffic. He could have taken my phone, leaving me with no way to get help. I could have run into him again. None of that actually happened, but these nightmarish scenes would flash through my mind in the night and suddenly I'd be wide awake, heart pounding, mouth dry. It took me months to feel okay on the subway alone.

I'm no idealist; I also know there is misogyny without men. Once on a date to a party, a friend of the woman I was with pushed me against the wall and licked my whole neck, telling me I should ditch her friend and come home with her instead. I had to push her off me and when I told my date about it, she was pissed that her friend had violated some sort of butch bro code, but not that she'd violated *me*. Another masculine-of-center woman I briefly dated told me that my catcalling problem was because "you're hot, babe," and that I should take the compliment. And yet another butch woman I dated swore up and down that queer femmes were more sexually aggressive than anyone else based on the liberties they'd taken so frequently with her body. I've known lesbians to only lust after straight women because of the idea of a conquest. And conversely I've had straight women push themselves onto me without regard for my consent, assuming that all lesbians are attracted to all women all the time. I once went on a date with a nonbinary dyke who, mid–first make out, suddenly bit my neck so hard they ripped part of a mole off with their teeth, but I was so high I didn't feel it, just sensed something was off and made an excuse to leave.

When I got home, I found my white T-shirt covered in blood, the beauty mark that sits near my collarbone partially dangling. Did they do it on purpose? And if not, why didn't they say anything about making me bleed? It was devastating to realize that the queer world was not without violence.

Similarly, I always wanted women's media to be a place where we were safe, but historically it hasn't been that at all. The problem wasn't just that men controlled most of women's media, though that was a huge part of it. The more insidious issue was that women had so internalized the policing of our bodies that, given a space just for us, writers and editors fat-shamed and slut-shamed and generally made women feel broken in order to sell pages. And even in the late aughts, when people were starting to grow woke, I remember a particularly breathless article in *Seventeen* with the headline "My *Boyfriend* Turned Out to Be a Girl!," which reinforced the point that women's media was not a safe place for queer people, in case anyone was still wondering.

Right when I started working at *Nylon*, in 2014, the first-ever national study on street harassment was published. It revealed something any woman could have told you: that most women have experienced street harassment, that LGBTQ people are the group most likely to be harassed, and that it has a long-term negative impact on our lives. Fueled by data, the media started covering catcalling like the actual, serious issue it was, and women began uploading videos to social media of their harassers. One woman filmed herself simply walking throughout the city with a hidden camera, showing just how many times she was harassed by men. It went viral. Eventually people pointed out that all of the white male harassers had been edited out to create the picture that all of her harassers were men of color, and a counter video was created, showing how much white men do in fact harass women on the street. It was a hot, complicated topic.

My boss Leila and I wanted to make a video about it, too. We set up a meeting with our video team, which was two straight white guys. Having a video address such a topical theme seemed like a no-brainer, but to my dismay, we couldn't convince them to make it. They just didn't think it was a big enough issue. One of them told us that his girlfriend, who was "very beautiful," absolutely never got harassed, so it really must not be a problem for other people. I think my eyebrows hit the ceiling. Not understanding what he'd said that was offensive, he followed up with, "I didn't mean to imply that you all aren't beautiful, too."

Eventually I had to bow out of the conversation because I was too mad. What they landed on was a series on sex; they'd cast "real women" and have them tell unfiltered stories about their sex lives, talking about taboo things like period sex. It was a good idea, one that would definitely drive traffic, but on the first day of filming I walked into the studio to find an all-male crew: camera guys, sound guys, male director, and a man who was going to be conducting the interviews. It was set up, basically, like an interrogation, with the all-male crew facing a woman sitting on a chair, alone. I intercepted, telling them it was unacceptable to have a series about female sexuality created under those circumstances. The compromise was that I would be the one to conduct the interviews. Sitting on an apple box beneath a camera operated by a man, I tried to maintain eye contact with the subjects, beaming an invisible force field around us that might somehow render the space safe to be vulnerable. I had no power to tell them to stop filming until an appropriate crew was put in place; I was just a senior editor and didn't oversee the video team. But it was a small victory.

That experience was one of the first times I started to suspect that what I really wanted was final say over the way all of our content was made. It was hard to stomach the fact that my strongly held convictions could be dismissed. And in general, how broken mainstream women's media was is why I wanted to work in the field in the first place. I desperately wanted mediums where femininity equaled power, not weakness; where the things that marked you a woman were the reasons you could enter, not the reasons you weren't safe; where women had the agency to define their own lives; and where no one would judge you for your aesthetic or who you loved. And I've watched the industry become close to that, and I've been lucky enough to be one of the entitled millennials who have successfully demanded more from the articles we read and the photos we look at. Because really, that's what all the men who have accused me of being entitled have meant: that I feel entitled to being treated equally, to being safe in public, to not just survive as a woman but to enjoy being alive. And for many of them, that kind of entitlement is so alarming it becomes an insult, hurled at me to try to make me feel small, but I no longer take it as one.

When I was in Texas for SXSW right after the Scorpio and I broke up, after I spent a couple of days hiding, I ran into my friend Kat. She's one of two friends from my childhood who turned out queer (you might remember Kat as the friend who taught me how to smoke pot after prom—the other you might remember as the best friend I kissed on a dare in high school). Kat was playing drums in a very cool indie band that was receiving critical acclaim, so she was there to perform. She had been on tour for weeks and was exhausted from sleeping on couches and floors. Over tacos from a truck, I told her about the breakup; she listened with a concerned face and didn't say much, but her presence was the most comforting thing I could imagine. My room had a pullout bed, so without much convincing she came back to the hotel with me and promptly passed out. I woke up hours before her and was fully dressed and caffeinated before she even stirred, but just having someone else in the room with me was all I needed to prevent me from continuing to lay there in my bathrobe, Gchatting my exes and feeling sorry for myself. Later, an aesthetician DM'd me on Instagram and offered me a free facial out of her home; she gently scrubbed my pores, professional affection that I really needed. And, that same day, I took a meeting with two PR people in the courtyard at the Four Seasons and ended up spilling the entire breakup story; they responded with much-needed pep talks about how I needed to start putting myself first. It turned out one of them lived near me and invited me to have dinner with her family. Despite how lonely I had felt at the beginning of that trip, I wasn't alone in the slightest.

And similarly, the morning after I was attacked on the subway, I had to go to Fort Wayne, Indiana. I don't know why I always had to travel right after traumatic things happened. Maybe I was just always traveling. At any rate, I was going there to speak at their Design Week, or DWFW; I was told that a group of local college students had specifically requested they hire me, and I never said no to young people. Going there felt surreal. I wore a red jumpsuit that I'd just bought in Paris, trying to look more powerful than I felt. The talk went well; to my astonishment there was laughter and applause, frequently. When it was time for audience questions, a young woman said, "How did you become such a badass?"

Still coming down from the trauma of the day before, I felt anything but badass. I felt scared and tired. And I was taken aback by the question. So I said, "I'm not."

I looked into the audience and could tell that's not what they wanted to hear, so I quickly backtracked, talking about how when you're a woman and you're gay, you learn early to fight extra hard for yourself.

Afterward, a woman who was a bit older than me introduced herself and then embraced me tightly. She said, "I've been reading *Nylon* for a long time, and I feel like I can tell when you started working there." She told me how much it meant to her to see racial diversity improve in the content. And then she said, "Are you hungry?"

I admitted, "I'm starving."

She, her sister, and her daughters took me and two of the other speakers out to dinner at their favorite restaurant. They told us about their work—they were community activists who had recently put on a gallery show about natural hair. I didn't tell them what had happened to me the day before, but I feel like they all sensed that I needed nurturing, because they carried the conversation, and they fed me, and they made sure I got back to my hotel safely.

I was so thankful I wanted to cry. That kind of support was more valuable to me than any kind of award or being on any kind of media list. And I know now, after years of therapy, that I am entitled to support, that I don't have to go through hard stuff alone—it's not a burden to lean on people who love you. If anything, it's a burden to shut them out.

In the taxi home from the health center where the EKG tech had humiliated me, the first person I called was my mom, who reacted with enough concern to make me realize that I hadn't been overreacting. She called me back moments later with my dad on the line. My dad is a doctor and was working for a corporate chain of urgent care clinics. Through his professional network, he was able to get the owner of that particular clinic on the line, and he made sure the employee in question was disciplined and that action would be taken by the managers. As an adult I've had a hard time letting my parents help me out, but it was such a relief to have them step in. Then I called my therapist, who saw me twice a week until I could talk about it without crying.

I'd started out my twenties desperate for independence. All I wanted when I moved out of my parents' house was to be my own person, self-sufficient and brave. But as I got older, I realized that my survival hinged on having a strong support network. I could not have gotten through that decade, and all the extreme ups and downs, without my family, friends, and the kind, generous strangers that moved in and out of my life. It took things getting really hard for me to fully appreciate the value of emotional support, but it's a mistake I'll never make again.

I'm lucky, though: I've never been raped. Or rather I've never been raped but I have a thousand stories of close calls. And really, show me someone of any gender who hasn't been raped and can tell you that without saying "but" right after. I'll wait.

10

The Cult of Empowerment

For the master's tools will never dismantle the master's house . . . And this fact is only threatening to those women who still define the master's house as their only source of support.

—Audre Lorde

In November 2018, I was contacted by two female entrepreneurs about a members-only organization they were starting for women in positions of power. They'd received three million dollars in funding to launch a women's-only executive network, and they wanted me to join the "founding class," the first group of people initiated, despite a waiting list thousands long. The purpose, they said, was to provide support to women who had gotten to a point in their careers where there is none: they can't complain or vent to the people above them, because it's usually just a male CEO or a male-dominated board, and they can't express how they truly feel to the people below them, because it's on them to set the emotional tone.

Women in power are lonely, they reasoned. I didn't need to be told that, but it was validating to hear. And, they continued, there's only so much venting you want to dump on your partner about your job every night. This group, with a steep entry fee and secret, chic headquarters in Tribeca modeled after an old boys' club, would empower women by creating a community of people in the same boat.

I said yes after about five minutes of chatting. I'd been complaining to my therapist for literally years about how alone and without proper mentorship I was. Forever lacking a filter, I told them, "It's like my therapist put you up to this."

Listening to the rules and mantras of Chief, as it's called, it struck me that there was something cultish about it. I got lucky: it is definitely not a cult. But it could have been: the recent headlines were dominated by news of NXIVM, a loosely defined wellness organization that claimed to be oriented around women's empowerment and instead was revealed to be a multilayered sex trafficking ring controlled by a straight white man that hinged on a female-driven master/slave system, which encouraged the women to brand each other and starve themselves. An extreme comparison, I know, but women who joined were lured in with promises of joining a supersecret, international women's empowerment group, so it's not *that* crazy to think about the similarities in marketing to commercial branding.

And it was branding that was everywhere. In the early aughts, as Ariel Levy famously documented, people began using the word "empowerment" to justify hypersexualized celebrity culture, using things like Girls Gone Wild and sex tapes to claim women's sexual freedom. And later, in the 2010s, feminism at its most corporate was manipulated to reinforce the oppressive beauty standards we only recently started to name, creating a cultural zeitgeist loosely based on feminism that appeared in branding for all kinds of companies. And it became somewhat cultlike: a cult of empowerment. But who benefited from it? And who controlled it?

It was a difficult line for me to toe. As an editor, I wasn't directly selling anything, but I did work for a business, and that business needed to make money to stay alive. Part of the way money was made was through audience growth, and my audience growth strategy was centered on wokeness—but the people who owned the companies I worked for weren't ever part of the groups I was looking to empower. In a way I had to separate that knowledge from my thoughts about my work, in order to not start mind-fucking about who was ultimately profiting from my endlessly long days and sleepless nights. At least it was privately owned and not supporting a larger, evil corporation, I supposed.

Once I quit my job and had some time to myself, I started to notice that there were countless brands that had begun to use the most basic tenets of feminism in order to attract consumers and remain relevant. I saw them on subway ads, in editorial articles, on Instagram. While I'd been putting my women's studies background into practice at media companies, empowerment had become an instantly recognizable, brand-able aesthetic. Cheerful yet minimal. Millennial pink. A certain set of alternating blocky and cursive fonts. Inoffensive, shareable, Instagram friendly. It had keywords: Feminist AF. Badass babe. Girl boss. Girl crush. Girl power. Kick-ass. Boundary breaking.

One problem with attaching such clear branding to an otherwise important and powerful movement is how easy it is to co-opt. Anyone can take these basic elements and apply them to any brand, and suddenly, at a glance, you can assume that their mission is vaguely related to women's empowerment, and that by supporting them financially or socially, you are in some way participating in the revolution, or at least, *a* revolution, or something adjacent to one.

Perhaps the grossest example of this is the way feminism has been repurposed by the wellness industry (if you can call it that—I'm not sure who gets to define what counts as "well"). There are the quasi-cults of SoulCycle and Equinox, which sell a hyperwoke lifestyle alongside high-intensity workouts, as though one is connected to the other; both are owned by someone who has helped raise money for the Trump campaign, despite the progressivism touted by the branding of both. And in connecting physical fitness to a political ideal, a new kind of drive is harnessed: the idea that yes, everybody is perfect and deserving of equality, but *you* are imperfect and the only way to fix it is by getting in really, really good shape.

And while wealthy workout junkies were pedaling faster and faster toward a manufactured feeling of empowerment at SoulCycle, other brands were selling feminism in a way that actively harmed consumers, like Flat Tummy Co, which sells dietary supplements that allegedly cause weight loss. It has millions of followers on social media and endorsements from various Kardashians, Cardi B, and even Amber Rose, founder of the feminist, sex-positive antirape SlutWalk rally. On social media, Flat Tummy Co's profile picture has a light-pink background and in white, the symbol for "greater than." The "real women" featured in before and after photos are mostly curvy women of color. The people in their ads, too, are women of color. In their text-driven posts, they call their followers "babe." Alongside saturated pink photos of women working out they have cheeky posts about eating tacos and burritos and drinking wine, lest anyone think that they're trying to shame you for eating. On their website, under "Our Mission," they list their values as follows: "We're real. We're relatable. We're inspiring. We're inclusive. We're supportive. We're empowering." Cover the URL and this could be the mission statement for a social justice nonprofit.

The brand, which was founded by a straight white couple,

started to make national headlines when it put up a billboard in Times Square blatantly encouraging women, or, sorry, "girls," to tell their food cravings to #SUCKIT by having a Flat Tummy lollipop instead of a meal. Aesthetically, it mimicked an ad for Thinx (the period underwear), and the verbiage was not unlike what you'd see in a newly feminist women's magazine.

It was widely accepted that the teas, powders, and lollipops the brand sells were essentially laxatives, which can be harmful to consume regularly and especially harmful to consume in place of real food. It seemed like a no-brainer that feminism and diet culture are inherently at odds with each other. And yet Flat Tummy's follower count—and revenue—continued to climb, a success that experts said was tied to an innovative manipulation of Instagram's algorithm to target twenty- and thirtysomething women in the US and Canada. If the words "empowering" and "inclusive" can be applied to a garbage fire of this magnitude, we're all fucked.

Few celebrities have been as publicly critical about Flat Tummy Co as Jameela Jamil, *Nylon*'s December 2018 cover star best known for her role as Tahani on *The Good Place*. That was one of the reasons I'd chosen her for the cover. I loved the way she repeatedly slammed Flat Tummy Co on social media with headline-generating captions like, "GOD I hope all these celebrities all shit themselves in public, the way the poor women who buy this nonsense upon their recommendation do." She spoke out about her own history with disordered eating and how irresponsible it is for celebrities to promote products like Flat Tummy tea to their impressionable fans. It was incredibly brave to be as honest as she was, especially about the over-photoshopping of celebrity bodies, and the silence from her peers was perhaps even more noteworthy than her messaging: the fact that no one else was yelling about it was part of the problem.

For our cover shoot, Jameela's management team made it clear that she did not want to be photoshopped. Jameela wanted us to know that she was proud of her cellulite and stretch marks and didn't mind if they were featured, a perspective that we all found inspiring. Meanwhile, though, over the course of production for the story, the internet at large seemed to turn on her; writer Katie Heaney tweeted, "I think it's okay if photoshop is your number one feminist issue if you're nineteen and in your first women's studies class. After that, it's weird." Dozens of media feminists piled on the criticism, critiquing the way Jamil was calling out women for being photoshopped rather than the people choosing to use the tool.

The irony, though, is that there was absolutely nothing that we would have retouched on her, anyway. Not that we generally did a lot of retouching (I too am adamantly opposed to it), but sometimes a celebrity would request a specific zit be removed or some such thing. In the photos, none of those alleged flaws—her cellulite and stretch marks—actually showed. Jameela is, objectively, one of the most beautiful women alive, with glowy skin that appeared poreless and thick wavy hair; she's tall and fit, too.

For all of her truly wonderful messaging about how everyone has flaws, Jameela herself appeared to have none. It brought me right back to trying to cast women for "My Beautiful Flaw" all those years ago. Her so-called physical imperfections didn't make her any less objectively attractive. It's a strange way to repurpose body positivity—yes, everyone is entitled to feel good about themselves, including normatively gorgeous celebrities. But that doesn't really do anything to help with the goals of the movement, which is about plus-size women and the discrimination they face.

Kristin Iversen, who wrote the story, brought it up to Jameela in their interview:

> I asked Jamil how she responded to people who protest that it's unfair for a woman who must know that she is universally considered beautiful to be leading the charge for a Photoshop-free world. She responded by kicking off her canvas espadrilles, and waving her decidedly un-pedicured feet in the air, indicating their imperfections, pointing out a specific toe as particularly unattractive. And she said, "My ass looks like a map of the world. I don't have a lack of gravity. I get spots. I have crooked lower teeth; I've never gotten my teeth whitened. I have cellulite."

Personally, I find the fact that she literally had to take a shoe off to prove that she has flaws to be equal parts funny and upsetting. And also, while Jameela cited her lower teeth and specific toe as evidence that she's not perfect, she requested that they not photograph her feet, and she smiled with her mouth closed in photos, and she wore a substantial amount of face makeup. As requested, we didn't retouch the photos, but ultimately, the parts of her body that she doesn't like weren't pictured anyway, so it didn't feel like any sort of big win for the cause.

In response to further criticism from other media that a conventionally attractive woman maybe doesn't have a right to criticize other people for being airbrushed, Jamil addressed the fact that retouching isn't just about looking artificially thinner and younger, tweeting, "But when you're a brown woman whose skin gets lightened and whose ethnic nose gets made smaller and who gets thinned out all without your permission making you feel bad when you have to look in the mirror or meet people in real life and you feel like a liar you maybe get my point?" The racism behind a lot of retouching decisions is very real, and I wish she'd discussed it more in our cover interview, or even at all. Women, at this point, seem to fully understand what is being done to celebrities to make them look superhuman; what's less discussed is the way Photoshop is used to obscure someone's race. For many women of color, that has historically meant skin lightening, and as Jamil mentioned, changing actual facial structure. For others, most infamously Kylie Jenner but recently a ton of white Instagram influencers, it has meant Photoshop and Facetune as an HD form of blackface, another tool for cultural appropriation.

Look: In the interest of the idea that we are all indeed just human, it's not really fair to expect an airtight argument from anyone for anything, especially someone who is a celebrity and therefore constantly under a microscope. I'll (thankfully) never experience the pressure she's under, and can't know what that must feel like, and further what it must do to your ability to be absolutely brilliant and succinct in your messaging at any given moment. It does seem like she is earnestly trying to do good; as I was writing this chapter, I noticed that a teenage fan had tweeted at her asking for advice on how to cope with suicidal thoughts, and Jamil had actually directly answered her, recommending eye movement desensitization and reprocessing (EMDR) therapy. And ultimately, as Kristin wrote in the cover story, "This picking apart of Jamil's physicality, whether due to a search for imperfections or as proof that she has virtually none, feels uncomfortably like part of the problem, and besides the point."

And that point, as I see it, is this: nearly all women, even the most universally beautiful women in the world, think that they have flaws. I've never met a woman who thinks otherwise. On another cover shoot featuring an objectively gorgeous young woman, we asked if there were any angles she'd like us to avoid photographing, and she said, "I hate myself from all angles, so do whatever you want."

In previous decades, this attitude made us easy targets for advertising language that promised to make us less flawed (and advertisements that confirmed we were flawed in the first place). In the 2010s and beyond, it makes us easy targets for faux-feminist branding, the kind that promises to empower us, to make us feel better about ourselves. It's the same message, just packaged differently. Corporations have learned the language of contemporary digital feminism, and they're using it to stay relevant to consumers who are sick of being made to feel worse about themselves. They're selling our own ideas back to us, as a millennial-pink means to an end that hasn't changed one bit.

In 1984 Audre Lorde warned against using the master's tools to dismantle his house. With the commercialization of female empowerment, though, the master is using the tools of the resistance—tools that activists spent decades fashioning—to build a new house, erecting walls and a roof around the movement so insidiously that we hardly realize we're being trapped.

And the master can take lots of different forms. Though of course straight, white, cisgender men sit at the top of our culture's power structure, other identities can do their bidding; white women, for example, continue to be agents of the patriarchy by refusing to prioritize racial diversity in their work, by calling the cops on black teenagers, by not believing survivors of sexual assault, or by voting for Trump. And women every day are starting their own brands using the language and aesthetics of empowerment in order to appeal to young, feminist-identified women, without ever making clear what exactly is so empowering about their product. It's the echoes of the parts of second-wave feminism that were found to be so problematic by lesbians, people of color, trans people, working-class people, and sex workers; it's Sheryl Sandberg's corporate rich white lady *Lean In* feminism, a flattening of feminist thought that neglects to factor race and class into a conversation about power and instead reduces people to just two categories, man or woman. And I don't think that being woman-owned and operated makes your company inherently feminist; the female founder and CEO of Thinx was eventually accused of sexually harassing the women who worked for her, after all (though ultimately the case was privately settled). Power is power, and if wielded for personal financial gain and little else, empowerment is nothing more than a marketing strategy.

I've often wondered, Isn't it good that Sandberg applied feminist ideals to the corporate structure? Isn't that at least a step in the right direction? Well, sure, sort of. But also, no. Sandberg's work at Facebook is certainly not a beacon of intersectionality, from what we continue to learn about its participation in the Russian hacking of the 2016 election and her knowledge of it, to testimony from black employees about the company's systematic racism.

The concept of empowerment gets extra confusing when you add in the layer of empowerment on an individual level compared to empowerment for all. Many fashion brands align with the former as though it gets them out of the latter, like

Victoria's Secret; as supermodel Karlie Kloss told the *Telegraph* in March 2018,

> There's something really powerful about a woman who owns her sexuality and is in charge. A show like this celebrates that and allows all of us to be the best versions of ourselves. Whether it's wearing heels, make-up, or a beautiful piece of lingerie—if you are in control and empowered by yourself, it's sexy.

But who, exactly, is allowed access to that feeling? In a world where consumers have been demanding representation for different sizes, races, and gender expressions, VS insisted on remaining a source of glorification for the same tall, thin bodies, with a product designed for them and only them. Despite that, it's another brand that claims to be empowering for women, because of the alleged result the product has on the individual wearing it.

The brand had also cited things like its admittedly decent racial diversity and how well paid the models are as evidence of how empowering it is. But there had never been any curve or trans models in a VS show, and many of their models spoke publicly about the starvation diets they were expected to adhere to in order to prepare for the televised show. Claiming empowerment under those circumstances was akin to gaslighting. And equating thinness to power was also eerily reminiscent of the values of NXIVM.

It was actually validating when *Vogue* ran a story in which, in a response to a question about whether the "Instagram generation" was looking for something different from their runway show, Victoria's Secret chief marketing officer Ed Razek came out and admitted to it:

> It's like, why doesn't your show do this? Shouldn't you have transsexuals in the show? No. No, I don't think we should. Well, why not? Because the show is a fantasy. It's a 42-minute entertainment special. That's what it is. It is the only one of its kind in the world, and any other fashion brand in the world would take it in a minute, including the competitors that are carping at us. And they carp at us because we're the leader.

Every time I read this quote I got stuck on the word "fantasy." It was so wildly illuminating. Runways had become the sites of fantasy for the rich, straight white men casting them. They were not for women. But they were trying to sell us something anyway. And *Vogue*, for what it's worth, despite being the outlet to publish the interview, continued to glorify the show, running stories like "The Victoria's Secret Angels Took Over the Plaza Hotel for an Epic Pre-Show Sleepover" and "Ahead of the Victoria's Secret Show, See Adriana, Bella, Gigi, Behati, and More Play Two Truths and a Lie."

It would have been so easy to react in a meaningful way.

Nylon's video team, too, had filmed a video backstage with the Angels, but after this interview came out I decided to kill it. Instead, one of our editors, Taylor Bryant, wrote a story in which she interviewed trans models about how that quote made them feel. Her ongoing coverage of the incident became our top-performing stories of the month. It was a no-brainer, and many women's media outlets made similar decisions, while people on Twitter and Instagram erupted with very appropriately directed outrage. It led to an incredibly important, internet-wide conversation about the damage that Victoria's Secret has done, and the attention began to shift to brands in the same space doing an actually great job; like Rihanna's lingerie line, Savage x Fenty. During NYFW in 2019, Rihanna showcased the collection on dancers and models of all races, sizes, and genders at Barclays Center in Brooklyn, and it was the most glorious celebration of diversity that I've ever witnessed. I covered it for *Instyle* magazine and concluded my piece with "Victoria could never." It was the final nail in Victoria's coffin, too: several months later, VS announced they'd no longer be doing their show at all.

Part of the problem is that these two universes—the universe of feminist-branded companies that are walking the walk, and the ones that are just using the words—don't generally seem to interact with each other. And when they do, in my experience, it's rarely productive; no one wants to be told that their version of empowerment is flawed. I've witnessed this firsthand many times, but one incident in particular stands out: A few

years ago I was asked to moderate a panel at a daylong conference geared around empowering young women in their careers.
It was at a beautiful convention center in Brooklyn filled with
vendor booths selling makeup and vitamin supplements, and
featured selfie stations that included a ball pit and a flower wall.
The other people on my panel were influencers, fashion bloggers, one designer, and one blogger-turned-designer. They were
all there because they were, allegedly, empowered young feminist women who were disrupting their industries and setting a
strong example for other women.

One of the questions I asked them, in front of a crowd of
several hundred people, was about copycatting in fashion and
how, if at all, that impacts their work. The designer was a woman
who founded her own company with the goal of helping create
jobs for women in African countries; her work is gorgeous and
very expensive, thanks to the way she collaborates with local
artisans and pays them fair wages. She spoke for a while about
how when fast-fashion companies rip off designers, it takes jobs
away from women. The blogger-turned-designer, who had just
announced the launch of her own clothing line and a partnership with a major department store, said something to the effect
of, "I don't know anything about that."

The designer became extremely upset. She was sitting right
next to me, and I could see her chest turn pink with rage. She
demanded to know how someone launching a line could not
know about where her clothes are being made. It turned into a

bit of an accusatory rant. The blogger, who was sitting on the other side of me, began to cry. I looked out into the audience and saw everyone with their phones up, filming the moment; the ones who didn't have their phones up had their hands over their agape mouths. As the moderator, it was my job to, well, moderate. I thought the designer was ultimately right but that she was being somewhat of a bully. I said, "Since it's possible that some people in the audience also don't know about where fast fashion comes from, could you recommend some resources?" I don't remember what her answer was, but I quickly changed the subject after she gave it. After the panel, the speakers fled, and I wasn't asked back to the conference.

A few months later, the blogger's debut line sold out within minutes of its launch. There's nothing I can find on her websites about whether or not she ever did look into sustainability of any sort, but based on the fact that it's allegedly the most successful partnership the department store has ever had, I have to assume that there's no labor- or environment-friendly way to keep up with the demand at the low price point. Worth noting, she was also one of the thinnest people I've ever met, and I googled her name plus "eating disorder" to see if she'd ever written about maybe a struggle with body image. Instead I found multiple Reddit threads picking apart her appearance, debating whether or not her skinniness makes her "perfect" or "disgusting." I wondered about the pressure she's under as the face/body of a rapidly growing fashion empire.

I wondered, too, about how much her own ideas of perfection are influencing the product she was selling; the pants didn't go above a 34-inch waist.

So how, then, does a brand go about setting up a structure for actual, true female empowerment? Obviously, under capitalism, there's really no such thing as ethical production and consumption—but I once got an email with the subject line "Empowered Candles for Boss Women" and I am sure we can at least do better than that. So I made a little checklist:

1. Is your staff made up of a diverse group of people, including people of color, LGBTQ people, women, and combinations therein? Are you treating them well?

2. Are there people of color, women, LGBTQ people, and combinations therein in leadership positions? More than one? Are those people of different identities from each other?

3. Are you paying everyone fairly, based on the work they are currently doing?

4. Do they have good benefits? Do they have parental leave?

5. Does the product you're selling actually improve the lives of the people who purchase or use it in a meaningful way?

6. Do the images you're using to sell your product show a wide range of women? Are those women paid and treated well?

7. Are you giving back to the community that you're making money off of?

8. Does every step of the production process use fair labor? Is it environmentally sustainable?

9. Can anyone of any body type use and benefit from your product?

10. Are the people financially benefiting from the success of your product also invested in empowering marginalized communities? What are they doing to show that?

It's not an exhaustive list, but it covers the bare-minimum feminist-oriented elements of a brand that can honestly say it's built on things like empowerment, diversity, and inclusion.

I wish I could say that I've watched women's media become consistently more empowering, but like everything, it ebbs and flows. Some companies have diversified their staffs and their content completely, while others claim to have done so but still have all-white executive teams. I could only control so much at *Nylon*, but I was ultimately lucky; the sales team checked in with me before pursuing leads with companies that we criticized. Still, I often lay awake at night worrying about whether or not our content was making the world a better place, or at least not making it worse.

There's probably no institution doing anything perfectly, no one single thing that checks all the boxes and should stay exactly as is. But as our understanding of privilege and equality evolves, so, too, must our language. I know that there are a ton of people who feel as I do. My hope is that these adverse reactions to market feminism and commercialized empowerment or whatever you want to call it don't end up circling us back to where we were before, when no one thought to be a self-described badass bitch or a boundary-breaking AF girl boss. Because ultimately, when you unnecessarily feminize language, it's probably counterproductive to long-term feminist goals. To paraphrase a brilliant point that Amanda Montell made in her book *Wordslut: A Feminist Guide to Taking Back the English Language*, everything from cute marketing lingo like She-E-O to more serious editorials about "women in music" serves to reinforce the idea that men are the norm, a neutral identity. Consider the fact that a title lacking a gendered qualifier implies maleness: a male CEO would never be a He-E-O—he's just a CEO—and a man in music is just a musician. The words we use to celebrate and then sell women's empowerment can also serve to hold it back.

But really, and importantly, it's not just an issue of selling empowerment or appropriating feminism to uphold beauty standards but the fact that our words can be used against us to justify all kinds of violence. I've seen phrases like "sexual agency" twisted to defend the legitimacy of a relationship based on statutory rape, while female antiabortion activists describe themselves as "feminists for life" and transphobic lesbians call themselves "rad fems," for radical feminists. The women who joined NXIVM called themselves empowered badasses as they starved themselves and blackmailed other women into becoming sex slaves.

I do actually think it's positive that we even created a feminist language at all, but if it is co-opted for other means—if our words turn out to be the master's tools—I think it'll be crucial that we not hesitate to create new terminology, a shift that will be, as Audre Lorde said, "only threatening to those women who still define the master's house as their only source of support." And this new language should invoke the feeling in the air: that real change is long overdue, and no one is going to make sure it happens but us.

11

Nobody Else
Is Perfect

There's an idea in astrology that when the planet Saturn returns to your birth chart, which happens every twenty-nine
to thirty years depending on when you were born, it brings with
it a period of intense, emotionally charged change, which in
turn leads to new wisdom and self-awareness.

I am actually *not* a die-hard astrology believer—I think you
can tell more about someone based on their thoughts on astrology than astrology's thoughts on them. But even so, there were
multiple periods in my twenties that I had thought might be connected to my Saturn return. My breakup with Avery and subsequent move to Brooklyn. My final recovery from anorexia. Maybe
my promotion to editor in chief of *Nylon*. Surely one of those

major changes would mark my astrological ascendance to adulthood. Finally I googled my birth chart to see when exactly it would happen, and it hadn't been any of those things. Saturn wouldn't return to me until January 2019 and would stay until October. At that point, I would have been EIC for over a year, with Wallace for a year and a half, and happily picturing what the rest of my life could look like counting on those two constants. I decided maybe Saturn return was a made-up thing and forgot about it.

After all, in January 2019, I had a lot more to worry about than when or if my Saturn would return. I was managing a team of nearly twenty people across four departments, overseeing a website redesign, and running a content schedule of twenty to thirty articles a day plus monthly cover stories. I had also just signed a contract to write this book—a lifelong dream, but I had no idea when I was supposed to actually do it. I'd written the proposal for it on the subway.

Part of the reason I was always so busy had to do with the small size of the company. It was all very DIY—literally. I was way more hands-on than other EICs, mostly because my team was so tiny that I had to be. And I didn't have an executive assistant. So much of what ate up my time was nebulous, things like schlepping to and from Brooklyn and trying to manage my calendar. I didn't feel like I could take any time off because there wasn't really anyone to do my job in my absence. So even though I knew I was hitting my limit, I tried to power through. I didn't see another option.

I thought I knew what busy was, but until the start of the new year, I'd really had no idea.

On a typical day, I woke up around eight a.m. and spent twenty minutes scrolling through Instagram. By the time I dragged myself out of bed and made it to the couch, Wallace had been up for an hour and a half. We drank coffee together quietly; I rested my head on her shoulder as my eyes adjusted to the morning light. I showered quickly and put on a fancy dress: on the day I'm remembering, it was long-sleeve and floor-length, with frilly tiers of fabric and a pussy bow, in a shiny yellow gold with an intricate pattern made up of abstract women's faces. We took the subway into Manhattan together—a three-train commute, the G to the C to the F.

I almost always had around five hundred emails by the time I got to the office, and this morning was no different. I got through as many of them as possible, then had a meeting with the marketing department, and then tried to read as much of the website as I could.

At eleven a.m., I ran over to Ludlow House on the Lower East Side, which was an offshoot of Soho House, an uber-bougie members-only global clubhouse chain. There, about fifty fashion editors were squished into an elegant room; there were racks of clothing along the walls, plush velvet chairs, and waiters bringing around teeny-tiny breakfast morsels, none of which I was able to grab. I'd been to this room before; last time, it was to meet Madonna and hear about her new skin-care line.

This time, a pop star was debuting a new fashion collaboration, and we were all there to see it, and more importantly, see *her*.

There was a small stage at the front of the room with a cluster of bored-looking models dressed in the clothes. Some were standing; some were leaning against props. They were *so skinny*. They looked like teenagers. I wondered what sizes they were wearing. Extra extra extra small? I wondered what sizes the line went up to. Either way, they were basically wearing yoga pants and sports bras, and I was fixated on their impossibly thin waists. The pop star, who had designed collections before, was infamous for casting models who looked like this, and I didn't know why I was so surprised.

I stopped gawking and checked my email on my phone. I'd gotten about one hundred more since I left the office. I scrolled for a few minutes and then looked back up.

One of the models was flat on the floor.

Two other models rushed to her side. A woman with a headset emerged from backstage with some orange juice. The model who fainted propped herself up on her elbows and took a few timid sips. I heard one of the other models say to the production person, "It's just really hot up here." I looked around to see if anyone in the crowd noticed. Most people were chatting with their peers, not watching the scene unfold on the stage. I saw a few other women quietly staring, but no one said anything. The models helped the other girl up and they walked her offstage; they then immediately returned to their posts.

Moments later a PR person appeared and everyone was quiet. She introduced the pop star, who came onstage with a friend. They were both, they told us, hungover from the launch party the night before; and they were both clothed in the line. The pop star looked like a beautiful, tiny bird, the smallness of her legs magnified by the spandex. I could see the knobs of her knees. After a quick chat, they took audience questions. Someone asked, "What part of your body do you love the most?"

She stammered for a moment and said, "Well, actually I'm very critical about my body."

She then tried to course correct, saying that probably all women are hard on themselves and that we need to prioritize being kind to ourselves and, more importantly, kind to others. She had not answered the question and had instead given us a motivational speech about love and self-love. After, she walked the editors in small groups through the collections. She described the colors as "biscuit" and "sunset orange." The clothes, as expected, were great: the kind of slouchy soft things that gave you that cool-without-trying vibe. I left immediately after, sick to my stomach over the poor model who fainted, and frustrated with the hypocrisy; how could a woman so infamously thin talk about how critical she was of her own body and the importance of self-love *at the same time*? And how could she in good conscience cast models to represent her brand who are so thin they literally can't stand up?

Later that day, I ran to a dentist appointment that I'd been putting off for months, followed by a fashion PR meeting, followed by some editing, and then I had one-to-one check-ins with some of my employees. One of them, the newest one, asked if we could capitalize the word "black" in the style guide. The only reason we hadn't done it was because we were following the industry standard, but I hate following standards and was more than happy to agree to change it. Another employee was working on her own leadership skills, and we went over an email she'd written to a coworker. Later, I reviewed edits that someone else had made on a piece because she was worried she was being too tough. By 4:30 p.m., I remembered to eat lunch, which I did while I checked my inbox, which had filled back up. A little before six p.m., I took all my makeup into the bathroom and tried to make myself look human using a piece of toilet paper as a blotting sheet and reapplying concealer.

I headed down to Chinatown, where a beauty brand's launch party was being held at a very chic bar underground. The brand's two female founders, who were very tall with long, expertly curled brown hair, were wearing matching sequin jumpsuits. They quickly made it clear to me that they were a couple, and suddenly I (a) understood why they wanted me there and (b) was definitely interested in what they had to say. They walked me through the collection; it was makeup, but each piece was tied to a sort of reimagined biblical story that gave agency and power to the women involved. I asked them if they were religious. They were, as it turns out, both Greek

Orthodox, from the same island in Greece, though they met on New York Tinder. A queer femme Greek Orthodox beauty power couple! I loved them. Their mission was to infuse feminism into the marketing of beauty products with stories about Lilith and Eve. The whole thing felt a little far-fetched, but compared to the fashion event earlier that day, I was delighted by the effort.

I then went from Chinatown to Tribeca for the opening night party of Chief. In the entryway I ran into a woman I'd met a couple of years ago at *Glamour*'s Women of the Year Awards. We latched onto each other as the room filled up with well-dressed women of all ages wearing totally fabulous outfits (though no one was wearing anything as brightly colored as me—oops). I was also wearing a small, gifted Chanel backpack, which kept getting caught on people as they tried to squeeze past me.

Finally, the founders of Chief emerged, setting up stools in the middle of the crowd of women. They introduced the special guest, and out walked Whoopi Goldberg. We all gasped and cheered. Whoopi talked for about half an hour, giving advice like, "Don't be afraid to say to your boss, *What the fuck did you just say to me?*," with an emphasis on the importance of saying it loudly and cursing. My feet were killing me.

At 9:30 p.m., I got a car home. I checked my email the whole way home, getting totally carsick. Back in Bed-Stuy, I stumbled in the door around ten and was greeted by Venus,

Wallace's sweet pit bull who was now also mine, who wiggled noisily around me with a stuffed lamb in her mouth, an offering. I kicked my shoes off and discovered that they had actually begun disintegrating, which was probably why I was in so much pain. I promptly threw them out. Wallace was lying on the couch. I took her face in my hands and kissed it all over. Then I ran to the fridge. She'd made pizza the night before, and there were three slices in a Tupperware container, which I took to the couch and ate cold while we told each other about our days. I was so tired that I couldn't believe I was still alive. We chatted for about an hour, petting each other and cuddling, and then got ready for bed.

I took a lot of measures to make sure I slept well: sound machine, humidifier, earplugs, expensive sheets, mattress pad, antidepressants, pot. And in that perfect nest with Wallace wrapped around me, I tried to breathe deeply. But I was already stressed about everything that was going to pile up for the next day and inevitably bleed into the weekend. I also didn't do a great job eating, and I was mad at myself about that. I didn't exercise, unless you count running up and down the subway stairs in heels. Speaking of which, my feet were still throbbing. My thoughts were a jumble of things that happened: The model on the floor. The pop star promoting self-love and leggings. Queer femme Christian lipstick. All the accomplished women at Chief in their beautiful suits. Did I say anything weird or awkward to anyone? What was I forgetting to do? Should I have thought to capitalize "black" when I made the digital style guide in 2014? What should I wear tomorrow? Eventually, mid–panicked thought, I passed out.

This, I knew, was unsustainable. I did not think I would be on my deathbed wishing I had worked more. I hated that I was working my butt off to be comfortable in one of the most expensive cities in the world to then only get to spend a couple of waking hours with the person I loved. But I didn't see another choice. After all, all the things I was busy with were so *glamorous*. I was meeting celebrities; I was making impactful editorial decisions. Surely I should just be grateful. And surely it was just one busy day.

But it was not just one busy day. Things got consistently more and more hectic through the spring. In April, I turned thirty, but unlike the previous year, we didn't take a trip; I didn't have time. Weeks flew by, and June was so chaotic that I stopped trying to find balance and instead grit my teeth and looked forward to July, which would, undoubtedly, be better. It had to be. It became a refrain—what I said to other people when they asked me how I was, what I said to myself when I got home after nine p.m. every night, so tired I could barely take off my shoes: July will be better.

Obviously, July was not better.

But first, June. There was a three-day trip to Puerto Vallarta, Mexico, to shoot a cover; the freelance writer dropped out at the last minute, so I stepped in to both creatively direct the shoot and also write the story, which I did on the flight home because I knew that would be my only free time. There were two more cover shoots after that. There was the *Nylon* pride party, which I was hosting and helping to plan. There was a morning spent guest teaching at NYU, panels to be moderated, an evening featuring a Q&A with me at an art gallery. My lower lip erupted into a cold sore. A few people on my team quit, and I dove headfirst into recruiting mode, filling every spare twenty minutes with interviews. The first draft of this book was due, and as I'd feared, I'd had to write most of it on the subway and in cabs on my phone. I was busy with, objectively, good things, lofty things. Time spent with notable people. Being interviewed for other publications about my work. Invite-only fashion parties and gay pride parties.

In the middle of the month, Wallace and I moved to a new neighborhood in Brooklyn. I didn't have time to take a single day off to prepare, so we packed everything up on a Friday evening, moved Saturday, and unpacked Sunday. I was back at work first thing Monday morning.

And then, about a week later, I got sick. Even though I had planned on just powering through the rest of June, my body said no. I tried to go to work and left early, twice. I had a fever and a cough, and my whole body hurt. I could walk but only very slowly. My head throbbed, and having the lights on made it worse. I was so pale I felt nearly see-through. I had to go to urgent care twice. I had crashed.

On July 1, there was a last-minute, mandatory company meeting, but I couldn't get out of bed. My boss—the son of the company's owner—called me about fifteen minutes beforehand to catch me up to speed, and I managed to croak "Hello" into the phone. My voice was shot, too.

What he told me was this: They'd made the decision to sell *Nylon* to one of our competitors. The new owners wanted our editorial, he said, so not only was my job safe, but it would be an incredible opportunity for me. I asked if he'd be staying with us. He said no.

I was so sick that it was impossible to really feel anything about this news except exhaustion. I was dialed into the meeting where my team was told about the acquisition and then the meeting in which they met their new HR person. And after that I spoke separately to the HR person about what they'd be offering me. Meanwhile, a major publication ran an article about the acquisition, and it said specifically that I would be staying with the company. The story was picked up by multiple other outlets, which ran my name in the headline. I was the news. But none of those reporters had bothered to ask me what my plan was.

I spent the rest of the day on the phone with my team. I had lost my voice completely and was speaking in a hoarse whisper, but even so, I tried my best to cheer everyone up, to be helpful and inspiring, to show them the positives. But my best wasn't helpful. I simply couldn't do it anymore. Nor did I want to.

I'd always been cognizant of the fact that *Nylon* wasn't my company, but somewhere along the way I'd started running it as though it were. Its success became my success. I saw no separation between how I felt about myself and how the public perceived the brand. And to suddenly have this major decision be made without me knowing it was even on the table was like being plunged into cold water. For the first time, I saw the situation very clearly: It wasn't mine. It was never mine. It would never be mine.

Leila texted me, "This is some classic Saturn returns bullshit, GK."

In the days that followed, I had dozens of conversations with the people who had bought us, and with my coworkers, and with friends in the industry, and I could very clearly see how the next few years of my life would play out if I stayed on. But even though I knew it would ultimately be *fine* if I stayed and set up shop in the new office and got to know my new bosses and dove into new challenges, the loudest, most powerful voice in my head was saying, over and over again, "No fucking way."

I was done.

When I started telling people in the industry that I was thinking about quitting, their reaction was, "But you're the brand." And for a few days that appealed to my ego, and I'd let them talk me out of it. But then I started to realize that while it was a fair point that the brand was me—I'd remade it based on my own values, after all—*I* wasn't the brand. I was my own person, one that didn't want to be bought and sold. One that was burnt-out. I agreed to work until the end of July to help with the transition, and that would be that. I'd end this chapter of my life and move on to the next.

I had saved a little bit of money, thanks to my book deal—and the fact that living in Brooklyn instead of Manhattan meant all my money didn't go to rent. I had started to think of it fondly as my "fuck-you fund," an emergency resource in case I got fired or needed to suddenly quit without a backup plan. I guess I always had a feeling that day would come.

I was at *Nylon* for five years in total, but it felt like three times that. As I tried to wrap my head around what it would mean to not have my job anymore, it was impossible not to think about everything I'd gone through while working there. I was hired as one person and quitting as another entirely. I was no longer the quiet, pink-haired, domestic-partnered twenty-five-year-old commuting an hour from Queens every day; the one who could churn out news posts and bounce around the city to events like it was easy; the one with no boundaries, neither personal nor professional; the one who couldn't borrow designer samples because they were too big; the one who had absolutely no idea how to ask for what she needed, or even that she was allowed to.

I was ending the job as a thirty-year-old who was tired of working myself to the bone only to not have time to enjoy my life outside of work. I had survived heartbreak and abuse; and most importantly, I had learned what my own limits were. And those limits had been passed long ago. And for what? So that someone else could profit from my work? I was too tired to be angry.

I felt like without my job, I didn't know where I began and ended. Who was I if I couldn't introduce myself to someone without saying my title? What was my value? My relevance? It was like all the resentment and frustration that I hadn't had time to feel for the past five years bubbled up to the surface at once. It was the same way I felt after all my breakups: sad that I hadn't spoken up sooner.

Meanwhile, my new apartment was huge: a two-bedroom with a full living room, dining room, and kitchen. To get so much space, we had to leave the deeply trendy area of Bed-Stuy where we met and venture south, below Prospect Park. When you move to a new neighborhood in New York City, it's like moving to a new state. Everything was unfamiliar, with its own rhythm and culture. It was humbling to realize that after twelve years living in the city, I still knew nothing about most of it. I had memorized every detail of the neighborhood in Soho where I'd worked, but that was such a tiny strip compared to the vastness of the outer boroughs; and my small corner of Bed-Stuy, which was gentrifying so rapidly you could watch it happen in real time, was not in any way representative of Brooklyn as a whole.

We had enough space in the new place to turn the second bedroom into an office, with two desks nestled into the corners.

Wallace started selling her paintings online, and I started the enormous task of figuring out what I wanted to do next.

I felt lost. Any sort of pride I'd felt at being someone with an established career was gone. I was angry at myself for not appreciating a regular paycheck when I'd had it. For the first few weeks all I could focus on were the things I missed: little things, visceral things, like walking into my office in the morning, hearing the quiet hum of typing, packages waiting for me on my couch, and interns looking up nervously as I glided by, my heels echoing down the rows of desks.

But even so, I knew it had been far from perfect. I burnt out before I knew about the acquisition, after all. I felt guilty for abandoning my team, but I knew that the best example I could set for them was taking care of my own self. And even though they often jokingly called me "Mom," they were not my daughters. I was not their mother. Nor their therapist, or any of the roles I'd let myself disappear into.

My friends started showing up for me in ways I'd never allowed them to before—literally, showing up to my home. Kat came over and hung all of our shelves. My friend Leah, who I'd known since college, came over and sat on the couch with me. Lindsey flew out from LA and stayed with me, and then Gabby did, too. Other friends said that they would come to wherever I was, and so they made sure that amid my flurry of meetings they could buy me coffee and snacks, and hug me tightly. My phone was consistently blowing up with texts and calls and emails. There were so many people rooting for me. Even though on the one hand I felt used, professionally, on the other hand I felt totally loved and supported. Dozens of people reached out to tell me that whatever I did next, they wanted to be involved. My family called me almost daily to check in.

I was sick for a few more weeks, and with no job to go to, I could let myself recover fully. I spent a long time on my couch in a nest of cough drops and tissues with the lights off. I only cried once, thinking about all the jobs I'd turned down over the years, wondering what could have happened if I had left sooner. After that, I did a lot of staring off into space, and a lot of accidentally checking my work email, hitting Refresh out of habit, feeling the comfort of my phone in my hand. I did things I hadn't done in over a decade, like watching TV at noon and not showering until dinner. At one point I went into my closet and touched all my beautiful clothes and shoes, wondering if I'd ever have any reason to wear them again. But for the most part I was completely sedentary. Wallace would leave in the morning and kiss me goodbye only to find me in the same place on the couch when she returned. I couldn't remember the last time I had allowed myself to just be still.

I wrote a resignation letter that went out in August and used it to talk about everything I'd accomplished over the past few years—my push for diversity, for queer representation, for size inclusivity—and what it meant for me, a young lesbian, to have had the honor of the role. By the end of the day it was published, I had more interviews lined up than I could count. And then, after spending the majority of the month resting, something miraculous happened: I started having ideas that had nothing to do with *Nylon*, or even with women's media, for that matter. Ideas that, in fact, would have been impossible to see through at my former job. I also started having vivid, wild dreams that I would wake up from with my heart pounding, soaked in sweat. I hadn't realized I had stopped dreaming, both literally and metaphorically.

Working to disrupt ideas of perfection in women's media had been equal parts rewarding and disappointing. It's a paradox, after all—the idea that the people who create content for other people should somehow be experts on perfection, when really we're all just humans struggling to reconcile what we've been told our place in the world is with what we want for ourselves. In reality there's no one who has the right to dictate how someone's value should be determined, whether they're saying it explicitly or implying it with how they choose to depict people.

But as the media landscape continues to tilt toward a strategy that listens more than it preaches, and as readers realize they don't have to be passive consumers of content that doesn't speak to them, I think the next generation of writers and editors will have very different jobs. Jobs that don't exist yet. The era of heritage brands dictating trends is over, and even the idea of mastheads in general will be discarded and replaced by a more democratic, horizontal system, where everyone's voice is valued. At least, that's my hope.

In truth, I don't know what the future of women's media holds. But I don't think the answer is for larger companies to keep buying up smaller companies, and I definitely don't think white men should continue to be the ones who own and control everything. No matter how well-intentioned they might be, they have no business making decisions about what kinds of stories will best serve women and marginalized people. It's an outdated model, and it's time to move on from it, before the medium renders itself obsolete.

I mulled over this while I lay on my couch in the days and then weeks after the acquisition. And in giving my body what it needed, my mind was able to heal, too, and eventually my entire perspective shifted. The future was uncertain, but really, it always had been and always would be. The best I could do was be honest with myself about what I wanted and act on that honesty. Whereas I'd always viewed the timeline of my life as inevitable, as containing events that I passively participated in, I could suddenly see each step of the way as an active choice, one of a series of infinite choices that could lead to infinitely different lives I could live.

I felt a new ownership of my existence, free from the limited definition of power and influence that had so recently defined me. There was a gaping hole in place of what I had thought I should want my life to look like. And in that empty space, there was suddenly room for everything.

Acknowledgments

In March 2018, I got an email from Nicki Richesin with the subject "Your Writing." She was a literary agent who had been following my career and wondered if I'd considered writing a book. Flipping my hair back and sitting up a little straighter, I wrote her back in minutes: Yes. Of course I had. In fact, I had an ongoing Google Doc full of overwrought notes about what the past few years had been like, and I sent it over to her. She helped me turn it into a book proposal, and without her belief in me, I'm not sure I ever would have had the guts to do it.

This book also wouldn't have been possible without the editing prowess of Michelle Herrera Mulligan at Atria, who, through long phone calls and kind words of wisdom, did so much more than shape my chapters. It would have ended on a much more superficial note if it weren't for the way she gently steered me toward self-actualization. Thank you also to Lindsay Sagnette for her early belief in this project (and me), and to Melanie Iglesias Pérez for keeping me on track. And thank you to everyone else at Atria who helped this book come to life.

There are two women mentioned in this book who were alive when I wrote it and died around the time I finished it: Elizabeth Wurtzel, who opened the door for women like me to write this kind of book, and Mama Cax (referenced as a model with a bedazzled prosthetic leg), who ushered in a new era of representation in the fashion industry. I was inspired by them both.

I owe my entire career to the women who took chances on me and advocated for me, a scrappy little lesbian with big opinions: Annie Tomlin, Megan McIntyre, Leila Brillson, Neha Gandhi, Mikki Halpin, and Michelle Lee, all of whom showed me what true leadership means and continued to support me even after they weren't technically my bosses.

Speaking of which, I never would have had the brain space to write a book if my coworkers hadn't been the absolute best, and I am forever grateful to the *Nylon* editorial, video, social media, and art teams, and in particular Kristin Iversen, who set the bar for all of us with her dedication, creativity, and general brilliance.

My closest friends, some new and some old, including but not limited to Lindsey B, Leah, Gabby, Mimi, Amy, Kat, and

ACKNOWLEDGMENTS

Moira, who are the coolest, strongest, bravest, smartest people in the world, have supported me through everything, including the writing of this book, during which they took turns listening to me rant about it and assuring me that it was, in fact, a good idea to write it.

My beautiful, brilliant, hilarious sisters Miriam and Julia were the first people I trusted to read this pile of feelings in its rawest state (which is definitely a metaphor). I am forever grateful to them for being my anchors throughout my entire life, but especially during this process. Ultimately I just wanted to write something that my sisters liked.

My mom and dad have been, and continue to be, my biggest cheerleaders. In fact, they've always encouraged me to write, and really I owe literally everything to them and the way they've consistently supported my generally unconventional trajectories without judgment. I'd be nothing without their consistent love and guidance.

And finally, my sweet, beautiful girlfriend, Wally, who made me dinner and rubbed my legs, who listened to me ramble and rant but also (and maybe more importantly) listened to my long silences, who read draft after draft, who held me when I was feeling scared and cheered for me when I was feeling brave, and showed me that love when it's real makes everything else possible.

ACKNOWLEDGMENTS

Moira, who are the coolest, strongest, bravest, smartest people in the world, have supported me through everything, including the writing of this book, during which they took turns listening to me rant about it and assuring me that it was, in fact, a good idea to write it.

My beautiful, brilliant, hilarious sisters Miriam and Julia were the first people I trusted to read this pile of feelings in its rawest state (which is definitely a metaphor). I am forever grateful to them for being my anchors throughout my entire life, but especially during this process. Ultimately I just wanted to write something that my sisters liked.

My mom and dad have been, and continue to be, my biggest cheerleaders. In fact, they've always encouraged me to write, and really I owe literally everything to them and the way they've consistently supported my generally unconventional trajectories without judgment. I'd be nothing without their consistent love and guidance.

And finally, my sweet, beautiful girlfriend, Wally, who made me dinner and rubbed my legs, who listened to me ramble and rant but also (and maybe more importantly) listened to my long silences, who read draft after draft, who held me when I was feeling scared and cheered for me when I was feeling brave, and showed me that love when it's real makes everything else possible.

About the Author

Gabrielle Korn is an award-winning editor and journalist. She worked in digital media for nearly ten years, after graduating from NYU's Gallatin School of Individualized Study with a BA in queer and feminist theory, and writing. She's best known for her work at Nylon Media, where she served as editor in chief, and Refinery29, where she was the beauty editor and, later, director of fashion and culture. She currently works at Netflix. Born in Rhode Island, she moved to New York in 2000 and never left. She now lives in Brooklyn with her girlfriend and two rescue dogs. This is her first book.